HOLE STUDIES

HILARY PLUM

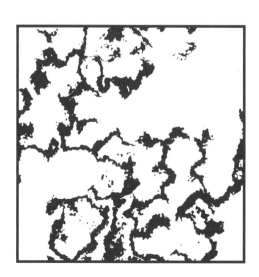

Fonograf Editions
Portland, OR

Cover and text design by Mike Corrao

First Edition, First Printing

FONO21

Published by Fonograf Editions
www.fonografeditions.com

ISBN: 978-1-7378036-1-4
LCCN: 2021951789

HOLE STUDIES

Fonograf Editions

To ZS & AP & JC

Drink and be hole again beyond confusion.

—Robert Frost, kind of

HOLE STUDIES

WORK, OR THE SWET SHOP BOYS

The page is flat. It turns or it doesn't.
The ceremony of trust requires no math.

—Paul Killebrew

I borrowed *The Eminem Show*—the CD, it was 2004—from my housemate, a friend. I worked in a back office, wore headphones. I got in around 9. My boss got in around 3. The floor of the warehouse we worked in was settling and to keep my chair from rolling backward I hooked my ankles around the legs of the desk. Eminem rapped about white America, a subject I thought I knew well.

It was 2004 and there was war in Afghanistan and war in Iraq. White America had started two wars.

There were four housemates, a kind of communal living thing that didn't last. We'd all gone to college together, an elite institution, New England. We lived way out in the country. Our landlords lived one hill above us, their yard scarred with several dozen car chassis they claimed they were working on. Dirt bike trails looped through the neighborhood into the nearest woods and at the foot of the hill a wooden cross marked where a couple dirt bikers had died. Our landlords' grandkids, we thought, maybe wrongly. The landlords would invite my Jewish housemate particularly to go to church with them. I thought he shouldn't go but he went. He was nice about things like that, too nice, he was from the South. I'm from rural white New England and if rural white New England landlords try to sell me on their white church I know what white expression to make, though I couldn't describe it.

My CD-loaning housemate and I carpooled

inefficiently into the small city we worked on opposite sides of. She was staffing a helpline at an organization that worked to prevent the sexual abuse of children. People called the helpline if they felt they were at risk of abusing a child. *A lot of people before you have burned out from that job*, her coworkers told her, or she understood. To help prevent burnout they'd redesigned the position, which seemed to mean that it was not a full-time job with standard benefits but a part-time job with limited benefits, though I believe they eventually added mandatory counseling.

I was working at a leftist publishing house, and Eminem was helping me correct a travel guide to Helsinki, or the index to a history of Hamas. Or I was checking the proofs of a debut novel by a Nigerian writer, my first proofreading assignment, and later I realized how much I'd missed, how much had passed me by. My lack of ear for Nigerian English didn't help. I was 22 or 23 and had a lot to learn about English. None of this was Eminem's fault.

The house in the country was on Sprinkle Road. I was often arranging repayment of my college loans over the phone (a landline): *Hilary Plum*, I'd say, *5 Sprinkle Road. So cute!* someone would say, and we'd set up a plan for me to repay my loans while making $11/hour. I was content with $11/hour. My previous wage had probably been less than $7. I paid off my loans within five or so years, partly from working but mostly from several small inheritances from elderly relatives, without which I would be in debt to this day.

Is any inheritance small?

I got up early. I wanted to do so much before I had to go to work. In the mornings I'd let my big dog out the door, and he—the only male dog in the neighborhood, or he acted like it—would trot out to the paddock where our landlords kept three old bored horses. Sometimes my big male dog would raise his nose by the fence while the old male horse lowered his nose. Noses touched. A patriarchs' greeting. It was early, misty. The wars outlived them both.

○

For two years at my last job I worked alone in a corner office my employers rented in a larger suite. The office building belonged to a private university that seemed to have bought out a quadrant of the city. Most of the suite worked for something called Business Services. Probably spreadsheets. My employers—a scholarly history journal, the job looked great on a CV, everyone reminded me—rented three offices there, but I only used one; the other two sat decadently empty while the suite's younger workers were stuck in cubicles. For two years the days were nearly silent. The six or seven people who worked together in Business Services rarely spoke. I'd never been anywhere so populated yet so quiet, other than in a public swimming pool, underwater.

Once I asked one of them, the friendliest one, if the music I played in my office bothered him. Oh no, he said, we all listen to music.

I'm telling you they were all silent.

Later some stray offices got rented to a teachers'
organization, and I would sometimes hear the man
who was the boss tell young women interns about his
youthful time on a kibbutz.

Upstairs was a sleep lab. People came and went slowly.

I was bored.

14

The job was 25 hours a week but there were maybe
2 to 15 hours a week of work to possibly do. My
predecessor had kept a pretty mysterious schedule,
and so there was an idea I should work regular shifts,
Monday through Friday, 1 to 6. Mostly I did, at
least at the beginning. Then I didn't. Mostly no one
knew if I was in my office or not, or no one I worked
for. The rest of the suite could have narc'ed to my
employers, but they didn't. They were on my side, I
think, if they cared at all, largely because I (a woman
in her thirties) was left to do the dishes of the senior
editors after our monthly editorial meetings, with
their ritualized sandwiches and potato salad. Until
the boss of Business Services said this to me about
the dishes, in a tone of decorous solidarity, I hadn't
even noticed this offense. It just felt natural to me to
do everyone's dishes. I was embarrassed, suddenly the
worst feminist here in Business Services.

I'd taken the job so I could stop working freelance, but I took freelance jobs again (more academic editing), did them while at my day job, got paid by two private universities at once.

Maybe it became my job to do everything in my life for which I didn't get paid while I was there, in my office, getting paid. I texted a lot, wrote long emails, received long emails back. I had long conversations. Friendships that had lain dormant, or never quite existed, or been nearly lost amid the *sorry I've been so slow to write back*s were suddenly vibrant. It seemed impossible no one could hear. I would leave to take phone calls by a fence enclosing a nearby lot that was becoming a parking garage. Giant black stockings filled with detritus snaked across it, blocking some movement of water. We talked about literature, for hours, not bored with any of it, not bored with each other.

My husband and I are part of a small press founded by two friends, all unpaid. I brought the novel I was editing to my office. The novel has eighteen sex scenes. I got flushed.

When necessary I tightened the sentences of history and made citations conform to Chicago style, Documentation I: Notes and Bibliography (not Author–Date). To drown out the silence I did listen to music. I didn't know what music to listen to because I have *no musical culture*, I might say, a phrase I think I heard Derrida say in that documentary about

Derrida. *But of course I listen to jazz*, I think he said. My relationship to music is sentimental, aiming to recreate a sense of promise and inchoate freedom I associate with dark late-night adolescent New England roads, the curves you try to take as fast as your friends. Beastie Boys, A Tribe Called Quest, Moby, Soul Coughing, fucking Blink-182. And college, the Strokes, sure, or *Kid A*, while around you everyone is dropping acid and playing bocce for days. (They're all lawyers now, or they run motivational programming for lawyers.) Musically I didn't know where to start and I didn't want anything in English. I can't listen to English while editing English, which is the only language I edit, and only partially, it increasingly seems. It occurred to me that although I'd worked in literature in translation my whole career (career?) I only ever listened to Anglo-American music. I can't read without reading critically, but I listen to music in some ignorant way, barely hearing anything, no craft. I doubt I know what's snares.

In the novel I was writing then I wrote the sentence: *When your husband is dying you get a job that pays better*. We thought then that my husband was dying. I'd dropped out of a PhD program I was lukewarm about to get a job that paid better, that job. In those two years my husband had two tumors, the second one perfectly visible.

o

My work life—like, maybe, yours—is built around

another, nonpaying vocation. Writing one, two, four hours in the morning. I try to be efficient. I arrive everywhere with my hair wet. My ambitions to have a job—to be, for example, an editor doing important editing, or to be a person who makes more than $18,000 a year—seem to conflict with my ambitions to do this not-job. You can describe these two ways to spend time (writing, working)—to spend or sell time—as if they made up one story, the story of your life. But in your life they have to happen at the same time. At that time you are due at the office. At that time someone is or may be dying. When I wasn't in my office, I might be at the hospital. I might be at my desk, writing. I might be in Microsoft Word's Track Changes mode, listening to an EP by the Swet Shop Boys.

What is it we need from each other?

What could we still make happen?

o

At my first ever job I did the dishes most nights. Dairy Queen. I was 16, 17, 18, 19. The controls on the hot water heater didn't work and the water could scald skin red. I don't feel much in my hands, so no problem. After closing we divvied tasks up, tried to finish as fast as possible. We got paid by the hour but if your shift clocked out slow when you next saw him the owner would raise an eyebrow.

Just after close, 10 PM, Big Steve would dial the local radio station to request "C'Mon 'N Ride It," the train song, so he could dance like a train while he cleaned the hot-dog roller or mopped the floor. "Big" just meant old—Big Steve was in his thirties, we guessed. He called everyone *chief* though no one seemed to like it. Hot Steve was a senior in high school and very attractive. When his girlfriend got pregnant he quit DQ to work demolition. People said you made $17/ hour working demolition.

When Big Steve got laid off from his second job, driving an oil truck, our boss at DQ gave him a straight-up $2 an hour raise so he still make his child-support payments. There was a lot of resentment. My friend had worked there as long as Big Steve and thought it wasn't fair he was getting a raise just because he was a dad. She had a point but I didn't agree. I was not very worldly, still virginal, and I couldn't have said what I felt: that we were sharing in an act of compassion for Steve's ex and kids. No, not compassion: responsibility.

Customers at DQ often ordered in Spanish, and those of us workers who didn't speak Spanish learned an in-between, ice-cream-specific language. Because I picked that up easily I assumed I'd learn Spanish naturally as I got older, but that isn't how learning works. DQ's workers were white, Latinx, African American, Lebanese American, Afghan American, that's just what I remember, I don't really know. It was what's called a *diverse workplace*. Phrases like that are largely formulated in workplaces that are not diverse.

Since DQ I've mostly worked in publishing and higher education, workplaces that are usually very white. The faculty are—what about the students? The editors are—what about the readers and writers? Who gets to decide if you get to work, and who your work is for?

Publishing and higher ed are so-called *white-collar industries*, though in the US many of those working in them—higher-ed especially, where adjunct instructors are nearly half the teaching workforce—don't make anything like a middle-class income.[1] As adjuncts (termed by our employers *part-time*) our jobs are precarious, low-wage, no benefits, little support, but requiring graduate degrees. Often we piece together work at multiple universities to make a living, maybe $20k or $25k a year. Those who have full-time or tenure-track positions make two, three, four, five times as much, teaching the same classes at the same institutions. Of course tenure-track faculty have additional responsibilities that every year, given their dwindling presence in the faculty ratio, fall on fewer and fewer shoulders.[2]

Some adjuncts are just as qualified as their tenure-track colleagues, or more so. Some aren't and wouldn't be considered for that kind of job—whose work they are, every day, doing. As an adjunct, sometimes I interviewed for tenure-track positions and found I was already more qualified for the job I didn't get than people interviewing me who'd had that job for years. In contrast, the standards for hiring adjuncts aren't that high. The more selective the institution, the less adjunct labor it uses. The more "selective" the institution, the richer and whiter its student body.[3]

The trend toward replacing stable middle-class jobs that support scholarship and whose workers share in self-governance, with low-paying contingent jobs that maximize teaching volume and minimize workers' power, has occurred dramatically nationwide over five decades and seems irreversible. Attempts to organize adjunct labor win local victories, but the cause hasn't won the interest of the larger culture, which seems hostile toward workers whose labor occurs in intellectual institutions and who could have chosen to *get a real job*, the sentiment goes. Or is it that teaching should be a labor of love, so it's impossible for the work of teaching, an act of love, to be exploited? Adjuncts are often called the *fast-food workers of the academic world.*

College instructors find themselves on public assistance, using food stamps, approaching or entering homelessness. The extreme inequality between the two types of positions creates an environment of scarcity, competition, humiliation. Full-time faculty may start to fear for their own job security. Increasingly overwhelmed with the out-of-classroom labor of the institution, while having little say in how budgets are spent, full-timers are made into ineffectual, or even hesitant, advocates for their part-time colleagues. You're meant to be grateful anytime a budget isn't cut or someone gets paid a living wage.

$1.5 trillion in American student debt, yet next to nothing spent on class after class. Where does that money go? You, the adjunct, feel caught up in fraudulence. It's a sense of hypocrisy you share in, standing in front of the classroom, encouraging promising students with mounting loans and complex family and health and job obligations to keep on working for their degrees. You believe in the class you're teaching. You believe statistics that attest to the economic value of higher education in individuals' lives, their *earning potential*. You rarely discuss how these degrees might fail to yield a steady job or a dignified means to participate in the life of ideas. Though the proof of this failure could not be closer at hand.

It seems you're still learning how this failure works.

The degradation of academic labor is a large-scale problem, yet it must occur in specific choices made repeatedly by individuals. Somehow over time across the country it is as if there were a mass agreement, as if every time you looked at a budget spreadsheet you agreed that teachers should be paid only $3000 for teaching a 15-week course, and that more and more of the instruction at your university—the mission of your educational institution, or the product you are selling to students and their parents—should be made up of this low-wage labor, performed by people whose names and faces their colleagues won't recall and which are less and less likely (given the exhaustion of their days, commuting ceaselessly from school to school, grading and meeting students in hallways) to be known in their field. How does this feel? Now that I am not an adjunct (as I write this I have a full-time, non-tenure-track position—still by definition contingent), I don't know most adjuncts in my department. We just never meet.

Guys would come around Dairy Queen, where there were always teenage girls smiling behind the counter, bare legs and matching polos spattered with butterscotch, cherry dip. It could have been funny, the tears shed over the years for these guys. We girls would hole up and cry in the walk-in freezer. *He said he was 18 and had no kids, but he's 22 and has two kids*, the lament went. I didn't suspect a thing. I didn't do anything. You shouldn't take breaks that long. You shouldn't get pregnant. But if you did get pregnant, if you did get thrown out of your house, your dad some kind of Christian minister, or just a deacon, you might find that before long the boss at DQ had made you a manager, though there had never been managers before. Comes with a raise. A lot happens but we have some choices. You might find her on Facebook fifteen years later, mother of two sweet girls and pursuing a doctorate at Jerry Falwell's private Christian right-wing Liberty University, you can't tell in what.

○

I say that I took my current job for the benefits. While my husband was close to dying, my job-that-paid-better still didn't have benefits. No health insurance. If he started to die again, if he could no longer work, if we ran out of medical and disability leave, I wanted health insurance I could offer us both. This was the responsible decision, for my family, which was the two of us. For this new job of mine we had to move cities, though we loved the city we lived in. But really I wanted this job, benefits aside—I'd been trying for years to get a job like this, and I wanted it, even though we had to pick up and move from a city that had kept us, unexpectedly, alive.

At this new job I would work with a close friend, an old friend with whom I often talked literature, with whom I already worked on the side to publish literature. I knew that a chance like this, to be two women working closely together in our field, in charge more or less of ourselves, would not come again. Now we work together all day every day. When I get into her car, a bag of sour gummy candy awaits me on the passenger seat. After work I go to her house, or vice versa; we exchange writing; we meet for drinks here and there, swearing about this or that email. When I covered her maternity leave at our university, I realized how able I was to assume her role and responsibilities. We know each other so well that we know how we are different.

Later I returned to the draft of the novel in which an avatar of my own husband was dying. Once he was no longer dying I didn't want to write about that, and now in the novel a woman is pregnant, on her own, in a state of love with someone with whom she will not have what is seen as a relationship. This *what is seen as* is what I'm trying to mean. A relationship has a structure that allows it to go on, emotions and responsibilities stable, expectations understood—a way to introduce each other, for example, to family, or to become for one another a family. There is a form, and the recognizability of the form defines this as a relationship. Otherwise what terms to use, what forms to try? How do I know who I could be for you? Through what work may we gain this knowledge?

Today my husband and I live in two different cities. Our jobs are now in different cities, and we both want or need to have jobs, or to have these particular jobs. It's a question. It's a common situation for those who work in *the academy* (over the years he and I have applied to other kinds of jobs, with no results). After years of cancer he is in remission, a state defined by lack of proof for its opposite, *no evidence of disease*. If the disease returns (it has returned before, from states like this), it will be because it was always there. Remission describes a state to be finally determined later.

To achieve this has required four major surgeries and two rounds of intensive chemotherapy. I'd guess the total cost was millions. Though the cost is never calculable; it represents an exchange that hospitals, insurance companies, individuals, and governments are continually in. We probably paid $15k, $20k, I stopped keeping track because it stopped seeming to matter.[4] I know that the cost of his survival was shared by strangers, not just through compassion but through insurance, a means to collectivize risk in order to equalize assistance.

Sometimes my husband will, at the end of the day, the end of the work week, tell me about something happening at his job. We're married, it's a thing people talk about. When I'm listening to a description of a task that I fear is a waste of time—normal bureaucratic assignment, sounds familiar—I feel an anger that returns me to any room in the hospital. I feel that if someone on the management level wastes his time, they're wasting the time of every doctor and nurse and visiting friend whose expertise and labor and care made it possible for him to be, today, alive and working. Each hour of his work bears within it these other hours. But then, I think—furiously I think—this is true of every one of us. Our labor isn't ours; it bears within it others' work, others' time, their years of frustration, boredom, achievement. And our work radiates through the living hours of those we in no other way know. You may feel what I'm trying to mean.

°

I think an office job—a boring, unsupervised office job—may be necessary for anyone who loves someone who needs care (someone ill, someone dying, someone just born). Anyone whom others call *caregiver*. And maybe for the ones who care for the caregivers. I guess the economy would suffer if we all stopped working whenever we needed to care for each other. But wouldn't we suffer less? In those years when I needed or wanted to be at the hospital, I went to the hospital. Sometimes I took proofs of the history

25

journal with me, though there was no point. It's hard to do that sort of work in a hospital, surrounded by the sounds and smells of the work a hospital is doing, and in my husband's room a TV playing a marathon of a reality show called *Escaping Polygamy*. On reflection that's a pro-monogamy message, though this wasn't the show's point. The show was about a group of women extracting themselves and one another from some sort of rural white polygamous cult. It felt clear that severe abuse took place in the cult that the show—for legal reasons, I figured—didn't describe. Or the show manipulated me into this belief. Its tone was uneasy, a contrast between the established genre of a reality show, the familiarity with which people narrate themselves to a camera, and the barefaced emotion of these young women, who had a guileless desperation the show couldn't tame. Of course this contrast was great to watch. During my work hours I came and went from the hospital or spent hours on the phone in my office talking to insurance companies, talking to the string of operators whose job it is to sound sympathetic—it's sincere, that sympathy, though I wanted to tell them not to be sincere, not to sell their sincerity to their employers for such a low wage—while blocking the progress of your claim. Even if your husband has been, for example, denied coverage for pain medication when discharged from the hospital, 69 stitches in his torso, metastatic tumor in the liver freshly removed. *My boyfriend's mother just died of cancer*, an operator told me, sympathetically, her sympathy becoming a tool her employers exploited, my husband's prescription forever denied.

°

While editing I can sometimes listen to hip-hop when I can't otherwise listen to music in English. The beat keeps the language I'm hearing from blending with the language I'm paid to read. Different modes of editing require different levels of attention; sometimes you want your reading mind to be lightly distracted, so that instead of following narrative or argument you are attuned to pure error, moving through minute units of language and watching as they assemble, again and again, into machines that mean. You want to see if any part fails to slide into place. To see this you don't attend to what the whole is gradually doing.

In that silent office when I first heard the Swet Shop Boys, when I clicked on the link for the album *Cashmere*, what I noticed, with distracted wonder, was the difference between the Englishes of the two MCs. The Swet Shop Boys are two rappers, Heems and Riz MC, and producer Redinho. Heems is Himanshu Suri, formerly of Das Racist; Riz MC is Riz (full name Rizwan) Ahmed, the actor; Redinho is aka Tom Calvert. Heems is American, Riz and Calvert/ Redinho British. In "Phone Tap" Heems gives some background: "His family from India but Riz Pakistani / My family from Pakistan I'm Hindu Punjabi." Often their songs have a call-and-response structure, alternating between MCs, and listening I blandly realized this is less common in hip-hop now than it once was, back in my Beastie Boys and A Tribe Called Quest days. There's a choppy/smooth shift between

Riz's keen rapid flow, with his forceful rasp and British accent, and Heems's round nasal lush American drawl. As I edited, Riz's rapping accompanied me, edgy and restless, the lyrics—quick wit, quick politics, interlocking multisyllabic rhymes   not quite arriving into the language I moved through on my screen. But then Heems's sly wide style would slap right at my attention, the big Americanness of his voice, his coy straight delivery sliding through ironic registers. In the specific environment of my editorial office, the delicate case of my professional mind, this shift among Englishes interrupted me, altered my listening. Again and again, a delicious surprise.

°

Surprise describes the beauty and risk of correspondence: how a note arrives in your inbox or crosses the screen of your phone and you can't predict it, a voice addressing you no matter what you are, in your own small life, doing. The voice sounds like itself; it's not yours. Surprise because whenever you send such a note you can't say how or if another might reply. In what forms does friendship happen? There's an ethos and an eros to the question. Correspondence is writing: it's the work of literature but not a product of literature. It's not concerned with production—a text that's known only intimately, not published, not for the public. Its language and thinking, the process of corresponding, informs whatever work you're doing, whatever day you're in, whatever books we may later, or never, read or write. But you still can't quite say: this produced that. There was no author, not even of one text or another, not quite; each act of language was a response.

In those years in that office I was a correspondent. I took on that work or the work took me from myself, relieved me of myself. I needed friendship and friendship was offered. A note arrived. What happens next? The question is a sensation of trust—next we will say something else to each other, we will be talking as we are now and yet differently, together amid differences to come.

Now I'm describing both a form of friendship and the work, as I see it, of editing. The editor makes a text into a site of dialogue, a place the writer is no longer alone. Editing is feared as intrusive, adversarial— the red pen and its violence; this suppression of the writer—but its work can be a rich collectivity. Word by word, sentence by sentence, I care for your work by dissenting from it, differing from it, responding to it. I build alternatives within and of it. This may feel like a release. I accompany you in the work, in its continual fearful flight from itself. I share my difference with you, and you with me. A book somehow results. But beyond the book lie hours of readers and writers attending to one another, together in a work in progress, meeting carefully in an unstable state. The greatness of this generosity is its risk.

○

"Post-9/11 Blues" was Riz Ahmed's first release as a rapper, a 2006 solo effort banned from UK radio play for its political commentary: "Post 9/11 getting around can be expensive / Cost twelve dead Iraqis for a litre of unleaded." In the Swet Shop Boys' songs, cops mirror and extend the imperial oppression served up by the "alphabet boys"—FBI, CIA, NSA, IDF, TSA.[5] "Counterterrorism" is a cover for racism, Islamophobia, fearmongering to feed endless war. Daily life under post-9/11 empire is subject to empire's necrotic militarized logic.

In a 2018 interview on the *Daily Show*, host Trevor Noah asks Riz how he thinks about issues of "diversity" and/or "representation" in his work as an actor. "I don't like to talk about diversity," Riz responds:

> I feel like it sounds like an added extra, it sounds like the fries not the burger... It sounds like... you've got your main thing going on, and yeah, sprinkle a little bit of diversity on top of that. That's not what it's about for me. It's about representation. And representation is absolutely fundamental in terms of what we expect from our culture and from our politics. We all want to feel represented. We all want to feel seen and heard and valued.

Not to be seen and heard and valued is to be killed.

"Think we're termites, wanna terminate us," the chorus goes in "T5," lead track on *Cashmere*. The lines before that were still playing, drawn out and sardonic: "Oh no, we're in trouble / TSA always wanna burst my bubble / Always get a random check when I rock the stubble." The "termite / terminate" line presents the stakes of the game. Riz's 2018 solo track "Mogambo" offers this bluntness again, defiantly: "They wanna kill us all / But they can't kill us all."[6]

To be denied representation is to be defined by necropolitics, as Riz describes in a video interview about "Mogambo":

> When you turn on the TV and you see a brown guy on it, nine times out of ten they're either being bombed, or they bombed someone… Either side I pick, I'm either killing people or I'm being killed. So in either of those outcomes, we just end up as the kebab meat, we're the dead meat to feed people's appetite in this war that's going on.

While listening to the Swet Shop Boys I worked for the private university that paid me and I worked for the journal it housed. The journal is prestigious in its field. The work done by its editors intimidates; anyone would admire their erudition, dedication, precision. As an institution the journal is, historically, immensely white and male. Of thirty-four editors on the masthead in one 2017 issue, eight were women. The authorship of articles followed similar demographic trends (over two years in which I worked there, sixty-three articles were published, sixteen of them authored by women; the overwhelming majority of authors were Anglo-American or European and white). Editors expressed concerns about diversity. Could these concerns become more than "an added extra," what Riz calls a "sprinkle"—could they become "your main thing," and how? Some editors proposed forcible strategies. In the meeting room one felt the presence of inertia.[7] The inertia of publications and structures like these is "white men," as the scholar Sara Ahmed defines them, as "an institution"; as "the *mechanisms* that ensure the persistence of that structure." "White men," Ahmed stresses in an essay of that name, means not just "who is here, who is given a place at the table, but how bodies are occupied once they have arrived"; "white men" is "conduct," "behaviour as bond."

"White men" still dominate the academy, its scholarship, its decision-making, the publication where I found myself as a nonvoting member. (Recent progress in the diversification of faculty—more women, people of color, workers from historically underrepresented backgrounds—has largely occurred among part-time, not full-time, ranks.) In my other field—trade and literary publishing, outside the academy—the institution of white men is now predominantly occupied by white women, or people like me, people I'm like. When I work, I work as part of a white majority built on oppression and over-representation; I'm within a self-protective whiteness whose exclusionary forces are at work.

Scholarship reproduces itself, recognizes itself. It recognizes reproduction of its forms. Knowledge made in the form of what it knows how to know. There's little opportunity here for iterations that differ; the form resists innovation—not like that, or not by you. To prove its significance, your argument must descend from and engage with the tradition of significant arguments, meaning the same thinkers, the same body of work, a whitened body of work that is accreted onto, made to increase.

It wasn't just the lack of diversity among authors published; the lack of diversity among thinkers discussed and cited began to wildly unsettle me. As I edited citations I began to note, without even wanting to (gender imbalance gets so easy to glean, skimming names), how rarely the work of women was ever read, discussed, referenced, or recognized as existing. In article after article, citations were relentlessly male, overwhelmingly white men. Canon. How rarely a woman's work was treated as meaningful. In my office, underemployed, husband in and out of the hospital, unworthy of this wealthy private university's health insurance, correcting others' writing so it would conform to the standards I had been hired to know, I felt the silence of these centuries of women. Felt, like a hand on the mouth. Where were their thoughts, their days and nights, the worlds they were building, their histories, philosophies, the frictions of their language, its private and shared forms? Who represented the dream of their living? Where the fuck was the world? Elegantly some machine recreated endless absence.

○

From afar a cemetery looks like a field of young birches.

But I was too close.

○

On slow days in the office I worked for a group I'd learned of through a friend, one of its cofounders. Together they or we ran a series of social-justice-themed correspondence courses for people incarcerated in our state's maximum-security prisons. Course readers were mailed out every six months, and participants proceeded through units of readings and discussion questions, mailing responses back to us. In that state, if you are incarcerated you are forbidden from corresponding with anyone incarcerated: inmates can't write to other inmates. One goal of the program was to provide, in spite of this cruel restriction, some forum for discussion. Volunteers typed up participants' replies to questions, compiled them, mailed them back out: below each question a half-dozen different answers sat next to one another, almost talking to one another. When your job was to type—to transcribe these handwritten responses— you had to decide whether to make any corrections, or "corrections," and which. In general we transcribers made few changes. You shouldn't change anyone's syntax, their voice. But—we wondered, and asked one another—should you quietly correct a misspelling, two switched letters, a word that was one word off in an obvious way? What would the writer prefer? To correct would be to standardize divergent Englishes, an act complicit with institutional racism, a subjugation of living variants of a language to the version the capital recognized. On the other hand, many writers might have wanted to have their spelling corrected, if you could ask them, which for practical reasons you couldn't. They might feel embarrassed to see someone had deliberately reproduced an error they'd made, just as my college students are often embarrassed, overly so, to find typos in their work and go out of their way to acknowledge errors of no consequence. Further, you might wonder if providing texts that lacked systematic grammar or spelling might be a disservice to those who wished to improve their skills in those areas—skills that enabled me, for example, to have the decent job I was, as I typed, exploiting. Further yet, any correction, any alteration, felt like a violation of the form of listening in which I was, as I typed others' thoughts into a discussion, engaged. But why should it matter what I felt, since I was facilitating an experience for others, not myself? Suspended in such questions was the power to identify and reproduce—or choose not to reproduce—the standardized majority variant of a language (a global, hegemonic language), and the indeterminate responsibility that this power entailed. In the silence of that office this power was my company.

Sara Ahmed writes: "It takes conscious willed and willful effort not to reproduce an inheritance."[8]

What body was I reproducing? Whose English do I enforce?

°

Like many adjuncts, I first taught college courses in composition, or *first-year writing*. Such classes, generally required, help students learn the critical writing and reading skills needed in college. The genre is academic writing, since that's the context (even at schools where the dominant majors are fashion merchandising, or dance, or graphic design).

Composition courses devote much time and energy to MLA in-text citation style. I always want to teach the principles of research and citation: as a reader and writer you're entering into an ongoing conversation; you have a responsibility to attend to and credit the contributions others have made; through this responsibility you may benefit from the work others have done. But I faltered when we got to the technicalities of MLA style, the quizzes on parentheses and periods and absent commas I was supposed to give. As an editor I regularly standardized and corrected the citations of established writers and scholars. In other words, the professors of these students didn't quite need to know, and regularly failed

36

to know, the sort of detail on which we were testing students. When a professor had a book or article accepted, someone like me would be hired to attend to those details, would correct where the writer had forgotten or diverged or erred. In my experience some scholars had perfect textbook citations; others were looser, or used alternative or idiosyncratic styles. This didn't reflect on the originality of their arguments, the accomplishments of their writing. Citation style is a knowledge so specialized a separate job exists to make sure it gets done. Yet we ask every student to master it and judge them when they fail. We invite students into unimaginable wealth—endless cultural work preserved, reproduced—on the condition that they'll be corrected when they don't perform this encounter in the form of our choice. At the cost of that little violence, entrance into this *discourse community*. But of course some will feel the sting more than others; some will feel more fully invited than others. And I will be the one wielding the red pen, a skill I have but don't need to coerce others to value. Or do I, to stay employed?

It occurred to me that if I could succeed in teaching every student flawless MLA style—if they then became scholars who could execute it without fail—I could put myself out of work as an editor. But no, to publish scholarship you need much more than good citations (though that was what our class spent time on). And anyway who will keep doing the hard work of scholarship, when, after a few more decades of adjunctification, scholarship is finally no kind of job?

○

To write her book *Living a Feminist Life*, Sara Ahmed employed a strategy: she refused to cite the work of white men. When I first learned of Ahmed's refusal, as I sat in that editorial office, I thought: if this journal tried that, even for a single issue. For a moment it wouldn't know itself. What would happen next?

○

Maybe that office job was boring because authors rarely disagreed with me. Editing is a back-and-forth, a conversation about how literary effects are made, intricacies of genre, grammar, possibility. It gets heated. Writer and editor don't agree with one another, then they do, or they split somehow the difference, or one disagrees with their own disagreement. The conversation takes months or years. Authors become your daily interlocutors, your friends, your beloved correspondents. But at the journal most authors were simply glad to have their language tidied and polished. Their priority was the argument and the scholarship it represented, not the sentences of which it was made. Their priority was the publication. Many were writing in their second or third language; I might rewrite a third or a half—maybe more—of their sentences, which were then correct, clearer, nicer in English. No one objected. They thanked me warmly, which I did appreciate. This was my skill; it wasn't hard for me. I did the dishes.

○

There are moments of encounter that expose the terms of encounter. We return to them because we are returned to them. Again and again in interviews Riz relates experiences in airports, where signs of Muslim identity are interpreted as signs of criminality. In these sites, where the events of 9/11 are nationalism's parable, he is read as potential terrorist, read as other, under suspicion of foreign intent. An early challenge, during an award tour for his role in Michael Winterbottom's 2006 *The Road to Guantánamo*, is prototype: an officer violently twisting his arm, violently asking, "Did you become an actor to further the Muslim struggle?" He says that for some time he felt himself, knew himself, in the terms of this stereotyping.

"I'm so fly, bitch / But I'm on a no-fly list," goes one Swet Shop Boys chorus. "Always get the random check when I rock the stubble," in "T5." Antecedents in hip-hop include the airport encounter in the 1999 track "Mr. Nigga" by Mos Def (now known as Yasiin Bey), or the trenchant ending—from stoner vacay in Amsterdam to locked up in Guantánamo—of Das Racist's 2009 "Rainbow in the Dark." Or the scene of interrogation implied in M.I.A.'s 2005 "Sunshowers"—"Ain't that you with the Muslims?"—a question Heems cites in the Swet Shop Boys' "Benny Lava."[9]

Riz speaks of this racism directly into mainstream

American cultural spaces—late-night talk shows, right out of the '50s—creating a potent friction of "de-colonial precision," as Sara Ahmed might say. On the *Tonight Show* with Jimmy Fallon, he tells the story of the "Ahmed 3," a parody of a boy band he and two other "Mr. Ahmed"s joked they could form when airport security summoned "Mr. Ahmed" for an additional check, and three men bearing that name booked on that flight appeared. The powers-that-be didn't know which man they'd meant, so searched them all. The Ahmed 3's first single, the short-lived band decided, should be called "Randomly Searching for You." Throughout the anecdote Fallon laughs a little manically, as if to insist he's in on the joke. From where I sit, he isn't. I'm not. ("I'm glad *you* find it funny, cheers," Riz says good-naturedly at one point, when someone in the audience preemptively laughs at his reference to being searched.) When I watch as this story is told, I start to smile—everyone's smiling—then pause, not sure what expression my face should bear. By now I've watched a lot of these clips, and through these repetitive interviews there's something hard to name in Riz's expressions: a grace prepared for the trespass of all these expectant faces. (My own.) That he shares this joke is his choice. That he wills this reality into a joke he'll tell.

I wrote a book that discusses my teenage history of anorexia nervosa and proposes the disease as a form of terrorism: self-starvation in the *land of plenty* as a terrorist form. The anorexic's protest is incoherent and literally self-defeating, yet its violence is unrelenting, self-sure, heedless of argument.

Anorexia nervosa involves a loss of self-perception, a loss profound enough that perhaps you can't trust your own seeing again. In those years I couldn't see myself as others saw me, which I guess is how you need to see, if you want to live among others, which is the only way to live.

Family works to sustain its children, to *put food on the table*; the anorexic refuses the fruits of that work. She presents an alternative ideology, in which dying is a mode of speech. She violates the genres of her own young life, inviting deprivation into sites that would exile it, making suffering and lack visible, asking death into adolescence and its promise. Anorexia is most often discussed in terms of body image, gender, dieting, media, looks. Sometimes personality, sometimes family. But above all it is about dying; it is a very slow, very public suicidality. Inexorably the anorexic resists domestic life with her dying; flagrantly she takes her dying out of the house and into the public world. Her extremity makes a stable cultural form—the dieting body, the disciplined body, the "healthy" body, productive and reproductive—into a mockery of itself.[10]

The anorexic is a pitiable figure. Wannabe beatific. Thinness is prized, but the anorexic, this good-girl student, learns the lesson so well she gets it wrong.

It's sad, her mistake, falling for the myth of beauty so slavishly that she misses the mark, dies. Her appearance gets read as a symptom of gender oppression, evidence of unrealistic, exacting expectations of gendered appearances, of the complicity of mass media therein. Though her condition requires great willfulness, she's often described as more victim than agent. This perspective is true, but incomplete. Its condescension is an act of mercy not extended to young men who participate in political violence. And it's a means not to read her meaning further, not to ask what politics she represents when she makes of herself something that resembles beauty but is grotesque—something that recasts her, in a domestic and global context, as a body with a different fate. Given a place at the feast, she chooses famine.

Today I sit and answer emails, I keep track of the tasks for which I'm responsible daily, I go on. Then, as a young teenager, I threatened to leave everything, I threatened to destroy everything by destroying myself in it, denying it the value of being worth living for, worth accepting a place in, worth taking part in, worth eating the food its global economy placed, to my very good fortune, before me. Worth nothing, no value. I'll prove it. Just watch.

Today climate change is a daily reality; the unequal history of mass consumption has an irreparably sinister tone. Against this background the figure of the anorexic appears, I think, as harbinger. As I left childhood to become an adult, an agent in society—

expected to make choices I would take for my own, to purchase this or that, to be known through money, through labor I sold on the market, the products marketed to me and which I purchased—I paused. I sought an exit, built a slow exit out of myself. Anorexia seems like a girl's misguided superficiality. But it is her excess of critique. She doesn't want to sustain herself here, in a place that promises unsustainability, inequity, denial, exploitation, freedom's opposites. Her protest is tragic, even amoral. But it's not meaningless. The potential of its meaning is ours to bear. She's trying to say something too self-contradictory for her to endure. She knows we don't want to know what she thought she could learn.

○

In my corner office the thoughts that occupied me, that fed my conversations, rarely touched the work I was meant to do there. My mind was rarely employed. I was very alive elsewhere. This was the hospital, the marriage, a book or two or three or a dozen, a poem you sent me, a book of poems, my own face in the bathroom mirror, a series of faxes I sent my Republican senator, Trump's Muslim ban and the spontaneous protests at airports I only read about, the end of a book I wanted to write, an article for a feminist journal on body cameras, a man singing to a man a poem written centuries ago for a mythic woman, a murmured argument, a book I recommended you didn't like, smell of cigarettes on my fingers, a happy hour or another, a benefit for an

Egyptian writer absurdly imprisoned for two years of his life, a book, a song, a poem, a book, a coffeemaker that overflowed repeatedly into a carpet I sudsily cleaned, another manuscript I printed illicitly, research on the Ferguson uprising you asked me to mail to your address in prison, forms of literature in which I was trying to live. When I walked back from the hallway bathroom, I forgot my face could be seen by others tucked behind cubicle walls. They could glimpse anyone who passed by. Did my face betray me, my distance from the place I was? As I was consumed—as we say—by my thoughts? What of my refusals were public, vulnerable, legible? Of what argument were they evidence? Your face appears in histories you won't write, can't read. If your face appears.

My father's job was the foundation of our family: what we were built on, built around. When he got a new job, we moved. For years my mother stayed home with us kids and worked part-time or freelance. For decades now she has been an adjunct professor of English, never tenure-track. I felt I dishonored her when I accepted this job myself, though she does it with honor. My father was a librarian, then a professor of library science—mostly in New England, but through various programs he worked and taught around the world, Vietnam, Kosovo, Georgia, Kyrgyzstan, Liberia, elsewhere. He left the house early, gave us a ride to high school, playing mix tapes my brother made, came home around 6, all day, every day, lunch packed by my mother in a reusable bag. He died of a brain tumor that slowly diminished his speech. When he was dying and expressed himself in gestures—a thumb's up, a wave—he kept trying to put something in his breast pocket, where you might put a pen or a pair of glasses. He was not wearing a dress shirt, of course, but a hospital gown. There was no pocket, but he kept trying, with any item you gave him, as if to keep it there, where it would remain safely with him at his office all day. A photograph my mother was trying to show him, of a field seen from the window of a house he had loved, or prayer beads my brother had taken off his own wrist. Later we might retrieve what he'd hidden there, where the pocket wasn't, next to his skin.

○

Is writing a political/activist act? a friend asked me recently in an email. *How?* He meant for me to answer the question publicly, in a video I'd make for his bilingual English/Arabic online magazine, based in Cairo. Because my books would be described as "political," it's a question I'm asked and ask myself. *I suppose I find myself a little bit surprised,* I responded in the video he'd asked me to make, *to be on the other side of having written those books and not feeling particularly more like an activist. Just feeling like a writer and editor and reader. But I suppose that's the work that I know how to do. Or that I've made myself into someone who does. I suppose the answer is no, that it's not activism, but that even though I'm kind of disappointed by that answer, I still believe in it* (literature, I meant), *for the ways in which its relationship to action, to the forms of the political, can't be pinned down, can't be described or easily known. And so when I think about… how I might begin to answer the question "what is the role of the writer"* (I seem to have replaced my friend's question with a different question, one my students ask) *for people who are feeling the urgency of that question, in political and historical terms, who are trying to respond, as we do, to history and the ruptures of history…* And here in the video I sidetrack myself into some of the events that have occurred since 2011, when I first met my friend (via email)—just after the 2011 revolution in Tahrir Square, in which he participated—and January 2019, when I'm speaking. I return to the idea that *what literature can offer is practices of attention. Literature keeps pushing beyond or through or dissolving the forms in which our attention and our language and our narratives and rhetorics take shape, and are disseminated, and establish themselves. So I guess that's what I want.* My meaning doesn't seem clear, though I seem confident my friend will know what I mean. Or at least that he will be interested to listen. *Correspondence*, I stress at the end, *is a practice of attention*. I describe correspondence as intimate, as collectively made, as outside the forms of production. I repeat something I've already said. I say: *And I think that's a good place to start.*

Riz Ahmed gets interviewed because he's an actor, that's the reason he's there, on this or that talk show. His music is mentioned, sometimes discussed, but it wouldn't get him invited into spaces like these. He works in one way that's prominent and lauded, and another that is, in his case, not as recognized; the fame born of one lends only so much limelight to the other. There's a sort of dance between cultural forms toward the center and toward the margin. In what moments or movements do you feel yourself in a politics you hope to share?

But now I'm exposing my own state of need, the questions I keep wanting someone to answer. I still want to know how work that's marginal matters, how publishing a book almost no one reads can be a meaningful act. The question is basic, embarrassing. When students ask it of me, I just nod. I just mean that I have the same question.

No, I mean that I trust them with the question. Our equality in asking it means there's a threshold beyond which they may learn what I don't know.

When I began my new job, I felt I became a new person. An aura of fraudulence dissolved. At the end of any day, having taught a class or two, having labored at a literary press at the university, a press meant to teach students the work of publishing, I have a feeling of having worked. On reflection, absolutely nothing perfect occurred. The feeling is its own reason. Some of the books I've published have sold only a couple hundred copies. Some have sold four or five thousand, or more, but how much more meaning is thus made? Some receive no reviews. Some receive great reviews, but if you're the writer you still have to do something the next day, have to find a new question, now that you've answered something so fully the resulting book no longer needs you. At the end of a day there is a feeling of meaningfulness when you offer detailed comments, a thick close forest of notes, on a student's work, even or especially if you reword those notes in your mind pointlessly later. Or when a chaotic class discussion concludes that pursued the unresolved possibilities of some text read together. You could never predict what someone would raise their hand and say. You couldn't prepare except by preparing some means to listen. Probably no publication will result from any of this, no recognizable trace. A book wouldn't get read enough anyway. Probably no vote was changed, no carbon captured. Later there's a grade, a degree, but just then as you leave the class there's no product. There's a feeling that people were meeting somewhere, that it mattered to us, even if differently, what we were trying together to do. Trying matters most because it's the most incomplete, the hardest to speak of—how much you feel its limits, how you don't know what it does. For a moment there was an opportunity—like a side effect that feels like the only cause—to care.

o

The EP *Sufi La*, according to a review by Mehan Jayasuriya, "serves as a reminder that Heems and Riz MC have range—that neither fit neatly into a box as joke-rapper or conscious-rapper." Are they some kind of "joke rappers"? When you sit down together with people for the purpose of watching the Swet Shop Boys, the Swet Shop Boys seem a little jokey. They're between something and something else. They're putting genre in play. "We're sad but we're stunting," they say.[11]

Joking lets you ask a question so that those with power might finally unexpectedly be questioned. Refusing a joke can work the same way. "To live a feminist life is to make everything into something that is questionable," writes Sara Ahmed.

(Maybe this is the part that's Eminem's fault, that terrifically angry clown—his rage isn't enough of a question.)

"Is this a joke that everyone thinks is a graduate thesis, or vice versa?" was the kind of question Das Racist faced—that one from an interviewer for the *Village Voice*, but the line got widely quoted. Not serious enough, or too serious about the wrong things? Who's the fool? The members of Das Racist were skeptical about how these questions worked.[12] People who like your jokes, who decide you're cool—they think you owe them something.

To question the security genre seems to offer, to shrug at genre right at the point of mastering it, to make a joke of the things you've had to sweat for. "A middle finger you can dance to," is Riz's catchphrase for his single "Mogambo." Critics comment on how in the Swet Shop Boys' work, humor and the party jam meet the political, how the group "capitalize[s] on contrast."[13] The in-betweenness of their genre identity seems to flow from the difference in style between the two rappers—as if the gap between them leads to further openings, a more contestable sense of space.

Examples of this in-betweenness are, say, in "Swish Swish" when Heems starts a verse, "I'm getting paid to lecture at unis that turned me down / Guap from Princeton, Stanford and Columbia." Das Racist got started at Wesleyan, a "potted ivy," I went to one myself. The joke is kind of on me, then; the joke is kind of on the genre of boasts like this, class-transplanted. "Uni" is a British/Commonwealth English word, not something Americans say. But Heems borrows from Riz MC's English, they meet somewhere in between—just as the personas they move through song by song are multiple, never meaning just one thing. Never unaware of how any real sign can get stolen, get sold (Heems's "You out of place like a brown Hare Krishna"; "… Hinduism in the bottle / Marketed and sold like fairness cream, that's the model"). In "Half Moghul Half Mowgli," Riz includes what seem like descriptions of himself from messages he's received: "Terrorist little Paki piece of shit" vs. "Because of you I went to uni, you're the man." To someone, this is who he is

Heems's lyrics have a just-rolled-out-of-bed quality: "I'm a cool guy, I'm good at rapping," he puts it in "Zayn Malik"; sincerity is another flirtation. Riz's style is about being one step ahead. In the *New York Times* Joe Coscarelli frames this juxtaposition as a working-class aesthetics:

> In the studio, the pair even found their disparate creative methods to be coming from a similar place of first-generation angst. "There's the working-class immigrant in me thinking, 'This is not a real job, so I've got to make it as complicated as possible,'" said Mr. Ahmed, who obsessively tweaks his rapid verses.
>
> Mr. Suri is more prone to trust-your-gut improvisation. "I go the other route: 'I should be working a desk job, so let me just get this thing over as quickly as I can,'" he said. "I don't want to have to think about the fact that I'm an aaar-tist."
>
> After all, he added, "What kind of kid from my neighborhood becomes an artist?"

When in my office I listened to these two voices pick up from each other, I thought without thinking about it: I'm listening to a friendship. Listening, you're outside this friendship and inside the music it makes, a product that feels incidental, trace left of a long encounter. No industry executive would have planned a product out of these two: the fit's not tidy. It sweats.[14]

Friendship tries amid and into difference; it trusts one moment into the next.

I think there are moments in which care discovers a form for itself, when care takes form. You might miss them if you're looking for something you expect. You might miss the responsibility you have to them. They seem to happen in an instant of questioning, of listening, of sliding out of some expectation, the beat after the punchline, a gesture, an expression, the pain or sweetness of being included in work no one could do alone. You're caught between yourself and a voice that's not yours, speaking right to you.

When "Mogambo" is released, Riz invites friends and fans, regular and celebrity, to join in: to record a video of themselves saying the movie supervillain Mogambo's tagline "Mogambo khush hua," which means "Mogambo is happy" or, depending on translation, "pleased." Mogambo is a definitive Bollywood villain, made popular by the 1987 movie *Mr. India*. Tom Hardy gives the tagline a shot, and so does Jimmy Kimmel when Riz is a guest on his show. The gimmick is simple but its stakes are significant: prominent Brits and Americans trying to get Bollywood right.

Shortly before his appearance on *Jimmy Kimmel Live*, Riz traveled to Pakistan, he says in the interview. His first time there in thirteen years. When he starts enthusiastically to describe the trip, Kimmel jumps in to say, "we hear things, and to me [Pakistan] seems like a scary place to go." Riz responds by citing Trump's recent speech in the UN, noting that "to a lot of people, America is a very scary place." Who is Kimmel representing with this interruption? He's speaking on behalf of a position he thinks he needs to accommodate: someone who couldn't hear Riz's story without their unwillingness, their suspicion, getting officially recognized. In the story that follows, alongside every reference to Pakistani police and military (he did run up against them), Riz includes a quick joke about the TSA, building an argument about how oppression works.

The two of them chat about the new single. Riz has an idea for a spinoff series in which he'd bring back the villain Mogambo, play the lead. Kimmel nods along, laughs, offers to collaborate, to play the part of "Mr. India."

Riz says: "Okay, let's do it."

"We can do this together," Kimmel says. And it sounds like he knows how all this goes, knows that moments like this don't need to mean much to whoever sits where he sits. *We can do this together*. But Kimmel could see, if he cared to see, that Riz isn't joking when he repeats himself—when he accepts what is now an overdue invitation—when he says again, just, "Okay."

HOLE STUDIES

NARRATING FORGETTING

It's hard to live now

It's the week of the fifteenth anniversary of the start of the Iraq War, if you mark the history of American violence in Iraq as starting in March 2003. After the sanctions of the 1990s, after the war in '91, after the Iran–Iraq War and the US arming both sides, after the CIA's involvement in Saddam's rise to power.

I'm reading Claudia Rankine's 2004 book *Don't Let Me Be Lonely*, a poetic document of the televised spectacle of the early Bush years, an American existence the poet maps through agonized presence, encounters with mortality, psychiatric medication. Late in the book this line appears: "It's hard to live now." *This line appears*: a book is always in the present tense, until the book itself is lost to history. The waters of the Tigris, we're told, ran black with ink and red with blood in 1258 when the Mongols sacked Baghdad and its library. This line appears in a passage that begins with the speaker trying and failing to get a cab: "At the bus stop I say, It's hard to get a cab now." A stranger responds, "say[ing], as if to anyone, It's hard to live now." The passage moves abruptly into what was then the current war:

> Hers is an Operation Iraqi Freedom answer. The war is on and the Department of Homeland Security has decided we have an elevated national-threat level, a code orange alert. I could say something, but... what is there to say since rhetorically

it's not about our oil under their sand
but about freeing Iraqis from Iraqis
and Osama is Saddam and Saddam
is "that man who tried to kill my
father" and the weapons of mass
destruction are, well, invisible and
Afghanistan is Iraq and Iraq is Syria
and we see ourselves only through
our own eyes and… the coalition
is inside Baghdad where the future
is the threat the Americans feel
they can escape though there is no
escaping the Americans because war,
this war, is about peace: "The war in
Iraq is really about peace. Trying to
make the world more peaceful. This
victory in Iraq, when it happens, will
make the world more peaceful."

The slippage between absent cab and distant war
is the writer's—the stranger has not said a thing
about Iraq; the scene on the street is American and
mundane—and is presented here but not commented
on. As the fact of race, the possibility of discrimination
amid passing cabs, seems present but not remarked
upon. It's hard to live now, but much easier at an
American bus stop than in Iraq. Rankine invites this
tension—exposing the American stranger's truth as
less than true—but notes it only by redoubling it on
a greater scale, by concluding with George W. Bush's
doublespeak ("the war in Iraq is really about peace,"
from a speech in April 2003). Bush's lie is grotesque

in its magnitude over decades and, as we reread his words, in our lack of shock at the lie.

Even the dead will not be safe
"We are in the summer of '91," the narrator of Etel Adnan's 2009 story "Master of the Eclipse" tells the reader. "Bombs are falling mercilessly on Iraq; the country is being destroyed; from the start the process looked irreversible and the outcome bound to be annihilation." The story follows a friendship between the narrator and an Iraqi Kurdish poet, from an initial meeting in the '70s to a literary festival in 1991, and then, after the poet's death but as his work has been seized on by an American professor of literature, into the present day, the newest war, the current war:

> Now, some fifteen years later, I am again hearing bombs falling on Baghdad. They are shattering my windows all the way here in California. Thousands of dead already and the war is at its beginning, and the National Library, with its medieval manuscripts, has been set on fire and a big chunk of humanity's memory has been destroyed; all this before large-scale killing has even started. Who is trying to eradicate the past and the present of the Arabs?

"My country has defeated Time," the American professor asserts. The dialogue between the narrator and the American critic surges into philosophy, mysticism, dream, an exchange in poetic terms whose balance is human life. "We made of the present our empire," the American says.

The narrator thinks of Walter Benjamin's *Theses*, and quotes: "even the dead will not be safe from the enemy if he wins." The angel of history hurtles through the last pages of the story—"that visionary angel," Adnan reminds us, "[who] is seeing the chain of catastrophes which affected humanity as the unfolding of a single and continuous event."

At the end of the story the living writer dreams of the dead. In a dream the dead poet appears to her; in the dream the angels the Iraqi poet wrote of in life are betraying him: "They are devouring me… they are starting to take my skin off, I am the meat of their banquet, which is being held by the Tigris, in the City of the Balance."

Out of every text, even his own, angels descend on the poet. As we read the dead poet speaks in the present tense; in the present tense he is devoured.

The dream of fiction imagines us into the endless present of despair.

The back of the hand

When I'm asked to go somewhere and speak of my first book, I find that I do not remember it. If I reread it, I recognize it—it's never a stranger to me—but I don't seem to know it anymore.

The novel imagines a group of friends, Americans of my own generation who make up a sort of new Weather Underground. Futile, inconsistently idealistic. To protest the war in Iraq they set off a series of small bombs. While writing the novel I would daily read news and reportage from Iraq, in this way bearing some form of witness, living a sense of implication that I felt these characters—imaginary subjects in history whom I created and then, to my surprise, forgot—should embody. Sometimes when asked I've called this a practice of attention. The novel imagined a tactic of American antiwar protest more spectacular than any that occurred. Its counterfactuality reflected back onto the apathetic contours of the factual. The novel became a means to know how absent interest in Iraq was on the so-called *home front*—not because of any lack of war but because, it increasingly seemed, few here wished to pay attention. Few of us "went there"; those few often went over and over again. For so many Americans, our presence wasn't required, our sense of responsibility suppressed. It was easy to live. Call a cab, get yourself home.

I spent four or five years reading and writing this way. When the novel was accepted for publication I felt a renewed obligation toward the sources I'd used. I reviewed the manuscript to make sure I hadn't somehow plagiarized someone, that another's words didn't appear somewhere unattributed in my text. Sometimes it was hard to tell. I could no longer remember which images I'd imagined and which I'd read of or seen on a screen. I'd read especially deeply Anthony Shadid's great 2005 book *Night Draws Near: Iraq's People in the Shadow of America's War*. There was one image, the aftermath of a bombing, that I believed I'd glimpsed in his writing but which I never found again. At around this time Shadid died. He was, as ever, reporting—this time trying to enter Syria, its uprising or burgeoning civil war. This was 2012. Readers have missed his reporting since, especially since we can't know what we've missed.

The novel was published in March 2013, the ten-year anniversary of the war. When I stopped writing it, Iraq disappeared from me. Not Iraq because Iraq was never present to me. But whatever I had practiced seeing—tried to see—was now obscure. If I didn't seek out news of Iraq I would rarely encounter it. Soon I found it harder to follow the stories—a few events occurred that I didn't quite grasp and then their effects were hard to comprehend. I didn't know what form of knowledge I'd had but I was losing it.

Soon the war in Afghanistan became the longest war in American history. The ongoing war in Syria began.

In 2013 my husband fell ill with a cancer that then metastasized. For some years he was receiving chemotherapy and our lives seemed to occur in the two-week cycles the treatment dictated. Every two weeks, start again. Sometimes I would have a thought, a phrase, that seemed worth writing down, worth not losing. I would go to my study and open a notebook and write. More than once, I found that on the facing page of the notebook I had written the same thought, a week or two or four before: the very same phrase that had just occurred to me. I hadn't remembered— I'd thought this was new—but there it was, in my own handwriting.

Perhaps what I mean is a line from the poem "The Stranger's Song" by Ghassan Zaqtan, translated from the Arabic by Fady Joudah: "And something of life on the back of the hand / was narrating / forgetting."

Later, in the days of Trump, Bush and his administration would be rehabilitated. Onscreen Bush looked gentle; now pundits appreciate him. They or we obscure the past, though for others it remains the present. Even many on the so-called left in the US seem to think there was more dignity in Bush's era than Trump's, more democracy, *norms*. They are not thinking or speaking of Iraq, or if they say the word *Iraq*, it is a synonym for American failure, not a place where Iraqis live and where American soldiers have very recently, most recently, killed thousands, hundreds of thousands, one million people. Lately the American left seems to use the word *Iraq* with a sort of inverted pride, as if this word proves they have always been right about what their country is. About who we are as Americans, though usually we mean other Americans, not ourselves. Here Iraq means the follies of neo-imperialism. Iraq means senseless, cynical tragedy. Iraq means lies and doublespeak and "preemptive strikes" and the failures of internationalism. Iraq means something Americans did. If you want Iraq to mean Iraq, a land and culture and history where the people of Iraq live, you may have a hard time.

In a 2017 essay, Fady Joudah describes this "default mode" of "necropolitics" as an anti-Arab racism that includes and allows for and extends beyond the case of Iraq. Joudah notes how "pro-Arab pieces" in American letters tend to be "pieces about Arab suffering and humiliation—that is, pieces wherein the Arab remains, with an air of inevitability, outside modernity, outside beauty." Through these representations Arabs tend to appear as already dead or less than fully alive, here and now. "Arabs are only alive on the surface of the liberal psyche," he writes: "They bob up bloated, are sometimes acknowledged, other times swiped aside."

At the end of the essay Joudah prescribes a practice for readers to counter the necropolitics and negative stereotypes of the Arab they ceaselessly encounter, to begin to know beauty and life instead. Repeat this line, he instructs: "The Arab is beautiful." Of this practice, he writes, "you will see how it changes you."

Try it now.

Peter Dimock's 2013 novel *George Anderson: Notes for a Love Song in Imperial Time* also prescribes to the reader a specific practice, a practice intended to "[rid] the self of its attachment to empire and [create] a true reciprocity of equal historical selves." The novel is a response—at once searing and intricate, impossible to live yet precisely envisioned—to the atrocity of torture perpetrated by the Bush administration throughout the "war on terror." Dimock presents this war's racism and torture within the larger history of American racism and imperial violence. The structure of his proposed practice returns the reader repeatedly to the acts of brutality and torture that constitute the history of American slavery.

"How do we devise a method for living the present moment within a frame of redemptive, universal history?" the novel asks. The novel is epistolary: the practice is being prescribed to a particular reader. This reader is a fictional stand-in for Daniel Levin, an attorney for the Office of Legal Counsel who played a significant role in the years of Bush's torture memos. Levin was brought on in 2004, in the wake of the 2002 memos that had authorized techniques long prohibited as torture, his task to answer the question of which techniques should be allowed, which forbidden. He undertook this task bodily. He requested that members of the Special Forces perform on him the techniques in question, and he declared many of them, notably waterboarding, to be torture. Yet the memorandum he wrote to convey this was undermined by a single footnote, which the

White House and CIA apparently insisted upon. This footnote effectively canceled the memo's arguments against torture and allowed torture to retain its legal status, thus shielding its perpetrators from justice. In the novel, the *you* addressed throughout is this lawyer, who is in the unusual position of having experienced torture, named it as torture, then extended its legal protection, allowed it to go on.

The novel's syntax tells us that *you* must be the reader; the reader he addresses is *you*. We are addressed in this site of complicit responsibility, compromised agency. "I do not know how to live this history," the narrator writes to his interlocutor, this agent of torture with whom he identifies, lamenting their shared place in the ongoing history of empire. "My complicity summons angels singing—I know that you and I are the same person."

Yet the novel manifests a radical hope. Sometimes on the left the work of literature is described as a form of *alternative history*. Future readers will know that in these days of empire, racism, corruption, war, despair, and annihilation, some offered voices in resistance, some gave form in their work to profoundly alternative values and visions. Alternative history: I have thought or said this myself. Yet what good is this? Instead I want a vision like Dimock's, in which there is a way to "[live] the present moment within a frame of redemptive, universal history." Literature is an alternative present you practice now.

"History is a discipline with which to dissolve an imperial self," the narrator of *George Anderson* argues. "History is a discipline to think from a place where you are not." In the novel this place is imagined as beyond imperialism, a "society of equal historical selves," a present in which justice, reciprocity, and love—love especially—may be realized. The novel knows that it doesn't know how to get there, but it senses this place may be both origin and destination. If you change yourself, you may see it. You may see how it changes you.

Love recognizes then changes you.

Readers will perform neither Joudah's nor Dimock's practice. Not to the letter, or not at all. Both writers know this, and yet both offer a discipline no one will follow. The space in which these practices take form is literature. The reader imagines what it would be to be the one who changes. *What if?* I imagine who I might be in a place where I am not. What language may be shared there? Literature is a place where you and I may still write our history.

What I never knew

In that first novel, characters read and discuss journalism from the Iraq War and, tentatively, they act in protest. My second novel extended this inquiry further into the act of reading: how do we read and write "news from elsewhere"? How may we recognize how subject positions and desires shape our media, our reading and writing? The structure of the novel hopes to illuminate the position and potential of the American reader in the global context of the "war on terror." Years of reading news from the war in Iraq had asked me to bear witness not only to the subject of war but to the ethics and limits of reading: the dynamics of perspective, subjectivity, unequal power, representation, and agency that we enter as we read. The novel is made up of places, conflicts, situations from all over the world that someone is trying to report on, to report back from—a fragmented multiplicity, a chorus of despair that cannot be wholly heard. I wanted to write a novel about a world amid this late empire's violence and also about the reader in/of that empire. The novel wants to bear witness to the limits of acts of witness, what these mediated American ways of knowing project and exclude, see and repress and distantly glimpse.

Through the years I wrote and revised this novel, I read not only journalism but more and more literature that was emerging from and speaking of this time, these wars, what it is to live now. Works like Wafaa Bilal's *Shoot an Iraqi* (2008), Khaled Mattawa's *Tocqueville* (2010), Julie Carr's *100 Notes on Violence* (2010), Jena Osman's *Public Figures* (2012), Rob Halpern's *Music for Porn* (2012), Philip Metres's *Sand Opera* (2015), Roy Scranton's *War Porn* (2016), Eric Fair's *Consequence* (2016), Hayan Charara's *Something Sinister* (2016)—a list that will never be comprehensive. One could always return to Etel Adnan's *The Arab Apocalypse* (1989). And in these years literature from Iraq that testified to the recent US war began to appear in English, including Sinan Antoon's *The Corpse Washer*, translated by the author (2013), Hassan Blasim's story collection *The Corpse Exhibition*, translated by Jonathan Wright (2014), the work of Dunya Mikhail, and more recent additions including Ahmed Saadawi's *Frankenstein in Baghdad*, in Wright's translation (2018).

While writing this second novel I grew preoccupied with how hard it was even to read journalism, a seemingly accessible genre: how much of the work of journalism the reader—and sometimes the journalist—may misread or avoid. The novel moves quickly among settings and situations in an exaggerated echo of the daily newspaper and its fundamental disorientation, where the story of a new US drone base in Niger yields to the write-up of a wedding in New York, which yields to a follow-up on the long water crisis in Flint. What happens when the reader accepts a brief paragraph as knowledge? What of the language of facts do we truly comprehend? How do we understand the partiality of our knowledge, and how may we act on that understanding? These questions begin with any reader and proceed through Trump's #fakenews. These questions begin in an appetite I too share. A desire to know, a habit of consuming something I treat as knowledge. I wrote the novel to try to learn who I am when I read.

In summer 2017 as I revised the manuscript, I felt how rapidly history was in motion. In its earlier versions the novel concluded before the rise of ISIS. A figure like Erik Prince, formerly of Blackwater, shadows the book, his private militias threading the map, his Islamophobia scarring the globe. In 2013, when I finished a first draft, Prince had nearly disappeared from American horizons. In 2018, when the book was published, he may have been at his most influential, his sister in the president's cabinet, his voice reaching Trump's ear. His proposals included using private forces to block refugees passing through Libya into Europe and establishing a British East India–style private company to administer Afghanistan and execute its war.

The novel includes a backstory set in the aftermath of Hurricane Katrina. In the week I made my last edits, Houston was flooded by Hurricane Harvey.

How to respond to this iterating history? How to speak of the "unfolding of a single and continuous event" we all may be living? Is the word surviving or dying or living?

"How can I remember what I never knew?" I wrote in that first novel, trying to see something of Iraq and the war my country was waging there, the violent history we were daily inflicting. This question belonged to many Americans: a coincidence of its language appeared, for example, in an essay by Philip Metres, titled "Imagining Iraq: On the Fifteenth Anniversary of the Iraq War," in which he considers the challenges of journalism and literature in the hands and minds of American readers:

> The answer to antiseptic coverage (Gulf War) or embedded coverage (Iraq War)… is not merely to provide images of corpses and flag-draped coffins, better body counts and eviscerated flesh. We need to unmake our own imperial narrative, to dial down its noise. Part of that dialing down will require us to listen to Iraqis themselves, who will help us hear again, to remember what we have never known, so that we might not repeat the disasters of the past.

In its original publication the text of the final sentence is a link, sending the reader to an essay by M. Lynx Qualey on "The Literature of Forgetting and Remembering in Iraq" (Qualey edits and writes "ArabLit," an exceptional online resource for Arabic literature in English).

In other words, the question isn't mine. The question means I need to ask the question.

The current war

On March 5, 2007, a car bomb detonated on al-Mutanabbi Street in Baghdad, site of the historic booksellers' market, famed as literary center. Thirty people were killed and a hundred or more wounded. Soon after, a bookseller in San Francisco, Beau

Beausoleil, began a movement called al-Mutanabbi Street Starts Here, which would eventually expand to include annual commemorative readings around the world, an anthology of poetry and prose, and other international works of literature, film, visual art, book arts, and translation. I've long known of the movement, but when I received an email in January 2018—a general encouragement to organize a local event in March—I was surprised. Is this, I thought, still happening? Of all the losses of that war, do people still mark and mourn that one loss? I heard myself form this question and found it monstrous—this lucky relationship to loss in which one needn't distinguish, one can prefer to remember vaguely the abstract, but not agonizingly the concrete, the absence here and now. I could see how I needed to remember here and now—how memory is a practice, a discipline that needs you.

I've taken this essay's phrase "the current war" from one of my favorite antiwar poems. "Yellow Rose" by Mark Leidner, from his 2011 book *Beauty Was the Case That They Gave Me*. "I am against the current war the most / because while it unfolds / I live, and I love / I suppose." The afterthought of "I suppose" is what makes the line so memorable—an awareness of the hypothetical quality of awareness, of the self's indefensible formulations, never separate from the vast brutal world. The poem realizes living and loving may necessarily, desperately, take form as a joke, a shrug.

The poem begins in the cruel pleasures of spectacle:

> When it snows I get a boner.
> Whenever those tornadoes on the news
> lay those colonies of mobile
> homes to waste
> I get a boner.

On the second page, after a pretty vivid list of things that give the speaker a boner or in whose presence "a boner's got," a turn occurs:

> and yet there are some things
> that do not give me a boner:
> the level of tranquility
> a Jeep of body bags achieves
> jostling off along a twisting gravel
> path, bound for home;
> the bracing red and white of flags
> crisply creased,
> handed over.
> Faces ceasing to exist
> the moment they come into being
> while a bomb is blowing up
> their neighborhood, people being
> shot like dogs, like nothing,
> nothing slumping
> on the ground, nothing blood
> is just a pool around.

The poem knows the American reader and her media,

who is seen and who sees, who lives and who dies: before you these distant faces only come into being as they are dying, as you take part in the pornography of their dying. At its end the poem returns to a joking mode it means seriously, evidenced by the phrase "to completion"—a sly joke about coming that serves as a gesture of longing and mourning:

> I am against the current war the most
> because while it unfolds
> I live, and I love
> I suppose. But who could possibly care
> what I have to say about this war?
> I could say anything here,
> it wouldn't matter. I could say,
> "I am Motortrend Car of the Year."
> Or,
> "You are the yellow rose
> corkscrewing out of the slippery rocks
> that gird the river of black water."
> "I have seen a thousand moons
> wax and wane to completion
> since we last touched."

Since we last touched. If we could touch. If we were here, now. These last lines point across an absurd distance to the love they still long for. To speak of that love exposes our futility, our hope, and our complicity in violence continually, spectacularly unfolding.

Insistent, desperate, Dimock's narrator writes: "I am requesting the touch of your words in the moving air (and the touch of your hand) in the hope that they will help me learn to live my complicity honorably."

Rankine's book concludes in a forceful state of presence, a state that asks you—the stranger, the reader—to join her. This poem, too, longs for and offers touch:

> … Paul Celan said that the poem was no different from a handshake. … The handshake is our decided ritual of both asserting (I am here) and handing over (here) a self to another. Hence the poem is that—Here. I am here. This conflation of the solidity of presence with the offering of this same presence perhaps has everything to do with being alive.

> … Here both recognizes and demands recognition. I see you, or here, he said to her. In order for something to be handed over a hand must extend and a hand must receive. We must both be here in this world in this life in this place indicating the presence of.

Here there is no touch, only text; the handshake remains figurative, abstract. Yet, the poem asks, what if?

"Your lover's window / has not slept / or overlooked you," concludes Zaqtan's and Joudah's "The Stranger's Song," and through the conflicting double meaning of "overlook" (to look down at, to see from above; to fail to see) the lover's gaze is both absent and present, both negated and still here. Love's forms are not always possible. Yet there are forms in which the impossible may exist.

Literature is the practice, I am learning, of such forms. Despair sings into the flesh and literature practices a form love may yet take.

.

1

I was the wife of a law student. One night I was surprised to find myself alone in the kitchen with the wife of another law student. The students were in the living room discussing some group project. The other wife was a Mormon, and I'd thought that we were such different wives our difference, not our shared status, would define us. But there we were, in the kitchen. We'd both married young, early twenties. She and her husband had started a family right away. She had an easy warmth and told me that she didn't expect to work outside the home ever in her life again. We were both English majors.

In the living room something familiar had happened and would happen again whenever you went back there. Law students were talking and you couldn't join in. You, a writer and editor at a leftist press, thought a lot about the First Amendment, you tried to ask a question, add an idea. About how the stakes of the case under discussion might shape society, the political world that this living room sat in. No. You weren't in the class; you didn't know the law; you had no role here. Somehow you'd assumed that what people wanted from a profession—the rigorous development of a skill set to be applied—was to connect that professional role and its modes to the world, realize its public potential. No. People wanted the professionalization. Its meaning required its insularity, its specialization was exclusion. It could be that this work was less meaningful if you, lurking wife, could join in the interpretation of its meaning. It could be that the institutional apparatus that trained people in this work just neglected the value of connection. You went to the kitchen, carrying dishes, where the other wife joined you, carrying dishes. Like you she was working as an editor, around parenting her young children, she'd picked up some editing work from members of her congregation. You felt a hard desire to distinguish yourself from her—how much more expert and important your editing work must be; how many years of experience you had; how good could she even be—then felt ashamed of that desire, I hope not too late, I hope before you let it be seen. If there are two wives in the kitchen, which one is the best? The living room might recognize one wife's potential, but surely not both. Is it recognition if anyone can get it?

2

Later I wrote a book about the Boston Marathon bombing. About how metaphors of illness get used in the rhetoric of the so-called global war on terror. The Boston Marathon bombing serves as a case study because it presented itself (to me, to everyone) one day as my husband (different husband) was getting his first cancer surgery. I was trying to relate the body to the body politic. We all have to live in both, intimately and collectively. The book draws on my own experience of illness and indeterminate diagnosis as a lens, means to examine how the radiating violence of the GWOT is represented in news media and felt by readers. How we encounter—and can intervene in— the ideologies sustaining that violence. After the book was published, when I was invited to do events or class visits, people asked me questions about the Boston

Marathon bombing. This made sense. Yet I felt myself in an argument, some state of minor alienation or non-recognition. I was an expert in form, not content. The book is a work of literature, not journalism or history. It's about structures of thinking and feeling and remembering and reading and imagining. Moving through it means encountering a range of subjects—anorexia; cancer; gun violence; veteran suicide; the Arab Spring—rendered with literary not historiographical or journalistic intensity. I don't know one thing about the Boston Marathon bombing that isn't in that book. I had built some possibilities for thinking about the bombing and using the bombing to think. This isn't the same as expert knowledge. I should answer questions about writing essays. *What can literature be a cause of?* This question appears in the book and so seemed like the sort of question that it might be right or useful to ask me, since it's the sort of question I had publicly, professionally asked. In classrooms people treated the form as a means to get at the content. I thought the form was a means to get at the possibilities of form, how form may allow for other new contents. I was trying to show how content *is* form. I believed this recognition could create new possibilities. But often people asked me about the book's content as if it was formless between us. I know about writing essays, I wanted to say, that's the main thing I know about. I really believe in the work of reading and writing and what it can do for all of us. If we're talking about any subject, if we're talking about what something means, we're talking about reading and writing and feeling and thinking and imagining, so that's what I'd like to talk about.

3

I'm often listening to Van Morrison's *Astral Weeks* every day. I mean my life has seasons like this. Once I was completely sober—it was morning—when I walked into the quiet kitchen and told my husband that the reason it's so beautiful, toward the end of the first track, when Van sings about being born again in another time, in another place—it's so beautiful because you know, from how he sings the line, that he knows there is no other time, no other place. He offers the idea of a time and place beyond this one because the idea is what we may offer each other. If there were another time, if there were another place… Sometimes—I often think, as I put the album on again—you have to get back to basics. You always have to get back to basics. Death is coming. All this complexity has the simplest end. There is no other time, there is no other place. Here you are.

1

Here you are, just you, stuck with yourself. Your work is never done. I find myself short on time. A feature of chronic illness and regular mortality. When will I read Foucault? I wondered for years. I had read Foucault, I think, when I was still young, but it must not count because I didn't seem like an expert, someone who knew. Around me in the city people seemed to know things. They had PhDs and wrote for *n+1*. I loved talking to everyone, even when I bitched about it after. I realized the solution to not having read Foucault was just to read him. An excerpt works. It didn't take long and then I dropped out of the program. I had been gathering context. Everything everyone had read made it into the soil of the air between us and everywhere, our jokes and backyard discussions, though I always went to bed before 1 AM, though the two of you were still deep in a passage by Ta-Nehisi Coates. I was nervous to talk about anything I might not know enough about. I didn't want to be a fool, but then I couldn't help it. When I heard academics speak publicly in that couching narrowing way of theirs—*well, that's not my field, so I can't really speak to it, and here are some people you could read on that*—I wanted to say to them: you're here. You're the one here. Be useful. (And you know essayists do this when we write *I've been thinking a lot about*… and then just virtuously mention a subject, not saying one thing of substance about it, moving on before we have to do any work.)

A fool is useful. A fool sacrifices herself. She'll give you something no matter her own expense. In Velázquez's painting *Las Meninas* (well, Foucault wrote about it), there's a perfect sly surprise: the portrait of the king and queen appears only in a small mirror centered on the far wall within the painting, while the face of the painter at work, the canvas of the painting within the painting, these are vividly near to the viewer, right up here. The artist shows us his own face, at work observing and rendering the king and queen who rule over him and everyone—and who are looking right at us, the painting's viewers, from their bright distant mirror. Anyone can see the painting on the internet, though some files are too low-res and the king and queen are blurred out. Anyone looking can see there's a game at play here, a serious game. Though the painting is from 1656, and we often treat history as simple and sincere (and a bit stupid, since they all lacked the internet). Most people know something about games and their seriousness, how you have to play to get at the real thing. For example, you can bring some experimental literature into any room, and people can and will read it and get what it's for. In the prison one day we read aloud together a couple of very short stories by Lydia Davis. At the end of one story—about how a character needs to feel superior to her friend without admitting she feels that need, since admitting it would mean exposing an inferior motive—E threw the paper in the air with a hoot. He shook his head. Well, that's it, he said, she said everything there is to say on that, that's how it is. I was happy because he was happy. A few years later the prison shut down our writing group. I had to write E a note (by this time he'd been transferred to a new prison he didn't want to go to and where he knew no one) to tell him I couldn't write him any more notes, which is what I'd been told. The reason the prison gave didn't make sense but prisons don't have to explain themselves to you. A problem Velázquez would recognize. Velázquez created a form of recognition you can still use. At the prison everything is painted a childish purple they claim keeps grown men calm. And where do you see yourself in 365 years?

5

Around this time we started listening to a podcast. Whenever we caught up with old friends we learned they too were deep into supporting Bernie Sanders's presidential campaign. The podcast was at the center of what was getting called the *dirtbag left*. The *New York Times* called it "rowdy, vulgar," "anti-establishment." One point of the podcast was not to respect the *New York Times*. The dirtbag left did not ally itself with the Democratic Party, mainstream media, respectability, incrementalist liberal institutions. The dirtbags had a form but they weren't formal; they had wide influence and reach but they were supported by individual subscribers, not institutions or corporations. They were called "Bernie bros," a category of supposedly toxic online young men (this podcast, *Chapo Trap House*, was in fact mostly staffed by very online youngish men). At the same time—for instance in 2020, as the Sanders campaign out-fundraised all other Democratic candidates, with millions of small grassroots donations and without corporate cash—you might learn that "'teacher' was the most common profession of donors [to the Sanders campaign], and Starbucks, Amazon, and Walmart were the most common employers of donors." It wasn't clear how all these teachers and low-wage workers were actually toxic online misogynist "Bernie bros," but anyway that worked to insult and dismiss them. The Bernie supporters I knew were poets, high-school and community college and college teachers, retail workers, editors and publishers in indie media, physician assistants, local reporters, emergency room doctors, psychologists who treated addiction in the unhoused, grad students, food servers, public-interest lawyers, undergrads, a guy wearing scrubs I talked to on the street, writers and activists against gun violence, writers on climate crisis, guitar teachers, freelancers, veterans, translators, education software workers, composers, potters, bartenders, unemployed, workers in nonprofits that served refugees, playwrights, parents, grandparents…

Toxic? Divisive? Unrealistic?

Medicare for All, a Green New Deal, a living wage, decarceration, an end to endless war, free college, student loan debt cancellation, taxes on corporations and the wealthy, massive wealth redistribution, campaign finance reform, gender pay equity, legalize marijuana and end cash bail, a livable future for Palestine.

A podcast succeeds because of form, not just content. Aesthetics make politics: dirtbag plus left, left as dirtbag. On *Chapo* there's a bro vibe, sure. Three to five friends chew through the news, analyze, insult the powers-that-be, heated, fast paced, always time for dick jokes, always plenty of interviews with leftist journalists, democratic socialist politicians, activists. In these forms of media, expertise is self-appointed, crowd-affirmed. No one hired you. Either people listen or they don't. They subscribe for $5 a month or they don't. There's no imprimatur, no masthead, no blue check, no way to prove you should be here, no credential, no CV gets you the job. In the last hopeful days of the Bernie campaign, February 2020, the podcast hosted an event in Iowa, gathering hundreds of people to canvass for Bernie in advance of the first big electoral test. Just before the caucus, at the end of a live show, they broke into song. At the risk, as they said, of being cringe. "Solidarity Forever," the union anthem, from 1915. The room sang with them. Listening to the recording you hear a cacophony of shouty off-key, out-of-sync, unpracticed singing. One host is yelling the song in a ferocious metal kind of way that sounds ironic but doesn't feel ironic. His co-hosts muddle the wordy verses then lean into the chorus, whose melody they can't carry. To hear familiar unbeautiful voices usually driven by fury, irony, despair, Weird Twitter, near-nihilism, desperate hope, relentless vulgarity, suddenly form a shambolic sincerity, a sincerity you might not recognize as such if you didn't know the usual mode, dirtbag context, was—as friends said who were there that weekend, canvassing and in the audience— shockingly moving. Listening, it doesn't sound serious. It doesn't sound like serious things sound. But it might make you cry. But Bernie won the caucus with the help of that room, its hours of phone-banking, door-knocking, leafleting, and conversations with strangers. Then, of course, we all lost.

Around this time I stopped citing. I lost some respect. I didn't need to show I'd done the reading. If I did it right you'd show me. I wanted to point to everything and everyone I partially, incompletely, inexpertly knew. I was writing this book, whether I knew it or not. I opened my mouth and kept writing. Most people who've ever sung that song are dead. You can only hear them if you sing.

O'Connor: *"I've actually lived for nearly 26 years and so [...] even if I had never read a book, which I have, you'd have to be fairly stupid, wouldn't you, not to notice."*

Interviewer: *"Not to notice what?"*

O'Connor: *"That it's all bullshit."*

1. Professional expectations

I've used the phrase.

I meant it. I think.

When you say something like that to someone, you're speaking to an audience beyond that someone. Your boss; their boss. A subpoena-to-come, a future in which you'll download all your emails as PDFs and send them somewhere to be judged.

To speak differently would require some form of mutuality that is beyond such phrases. The phrase *professional expectations* marks a failure of dialogue. It describes this failure as your interlocutor's, not yours. Your ability to use the phrase is a rhetorical parry through which you deny the possibility you erred. You're saying to someone: there are expectations—a code—you should know and you don't; you should fulfill these expectations and you're not. You're warning someone of their error's possible consequences; or threatening those consequences. But really you're saying (I've felt like I was saying): there's another way of being together, far from phrases like this. I'm giving up on all that, with you. I've failed to be there with you.

°

In a brief video from 2005—twelve years before the *New York Times* and the *New Yorker* began publishing accounts of serial rape, sexual harassment, and assault by prominent film producer Harvey Weinstein—a comedian hosting for *Comedy Central* stops Courtney Love for some playful chitchat on some red carpet. She asks Love (musician, actor, rock star, widow): "Do you have any advice for a young girl moving to Hollywood?"

"Ummm," Love says. "I'll get libeled if I say it. If Harvey Weinstein invites you to a private party in the Four Seasons, don't go."

She says it fast, as if tricking herself into not not saying it. She sounds like she's giving you something. Twelve years or so later, when public favor had turned on Weinstein and criminal charges were forthcoming, Love stated that after this tiny interview aired, she'd been "eternally banned" by CAA, the major Hollywood talent agency—which worked with Weinstein on many films and, though at least eight agents had been told about his abuse, regularly sent young women actors to his notorious private meetings. Punishment for this undisciplined moment of truth.

I once watched a documentary in which Courtney Love's own dad accused her of conspiring to murder her husband Kurt Cobain. Love is the sort of woman everyone feels comfortable saying anything about: messy, slutty, rambling, an addict, waste of talent, bad plastic surgery, whatever. Rumors shift credit for the songwriting of the band Hole away from Love and onto, traditionally, Cobain and/or Billy Corgan.

These rumors can be dispelled just by listening to Hole. An introduction to what we'll call Hole studies.

Courtney Love's speech that day was off-the-cuff, disregarded, prophetic. History proved its worth. For years Weinstein used highly repetitive strategies and scenarios, the hotel room setup especially. His crimes were both profoundly personal and systemic: by forcing and demanding sex "in exchange" for a successful career in the movies, and professionally punishing the women who distanced themselves from him, he set the terms for women working in American film. By no coincidence, the workforce of film and television has remarkably few women in positions of power or artistic independence; its lack of diversity, the sheer dominance of white men, is obvious.

But Love was not an authoritative speaker. In general—and especially when she suddenly broadcast this insider knowledge, ugly on a red carpet—she didn't meet professional expectations. I don't know if anyone ever took her good advice. Her accusation, not explicit but clear, had no effect on Weinstein's status. It didn't seem to inspire much curiosity or follow-up in journalism or among industry professionals—other than, like CAA, to punish the speaker—since twelve years and much more violence occurred before, from a more respectable realm of media, the story broke, or broke again, this time with the necessary authority.

○

Discipline finds you. Even if—up to the instant of transgression—neither you nor those possessing these *professional expectations* would have or could have said what they were. In March 2003, nine days before the US invaded Iraq, the country band then known as the Dixie Chicks (now the Chicks) were performing in London. It would matter to a lot of people that this happened on "foreign soil." In February a global protest movement, through the downtowns of cities across 60 countries, had surged in opposition to the threat of America's war on Iraq. The war was built on imperial winking lies, sold by President George W. Bush's administration: that Iraq had weapons of mass destruction, which it didn't; that Iraq's dictator Saddam Hussein had helped al-Qaeda attack the US on 9/11, also not true. That these were lies was an open secret, plain as day. But that didn't seem to matter, and the *New York Times* and others in media played along, running weeks of stories based on false rumors of WMDs—rumors it would have been easy to disprove, but they didn't. It seemed impossible that this war, based on obvious cynical lies, would happen. And then it seemed impossible that it wouldn't happen. That night, spontaneously between songs, Natalie Maines, lead singer of the diamond-record-selling three-woman band, took up the subject. To the crowd in London she said, in her Texas accent, her delivery understated: "Just so you know, we're on the good side with y'all. We do not want this war, this violence." Then she paused (in the video you can hear cheering), and of Bush she said, "And we're ashamed that the president of the United States is from Texas."

In the video she looks over at her bandmates and grins. She presses her hand slyly to her mouth.

Her life and career, the band's career, were never the same again. A massive industrywide repudiation followed. The Chicks' career was built in country radio; thousands of stations stopped playing their songs. They were blacklisted, protested, album and ticket sales vanishing. Demonstratively, in public, people threw out or destroyed their CDs. A sponsor deal with Lipton Tea ended. The American Red Cross declined to work with them on a future tour, reportedly fearing bad publicity.

These two utterances—Love's; Maines's—were spontaneous. But spontaneity has origins. There's some orientation, a mode of trust. These small speeches aren't revealing an inner truth of the soul, nor are they a plan of action or proposal, presented. They're about something public that's felt and said personally; they express the force of that feeling. The speaker's professional status enables the utterance: their profession is why they've got a mic and an audience. Yet for a moment they step past the expectations of that audience, the conventions defining the interaction of a performance; they step into some other flow. These communications speak from and expose a commonality that matters. Beyond the forms of my profession, she is saying, there's something that matters, and I trust it matters to you. Love seemed to be picturing—seriously picturing, in response to a joke question—the situation of a young girl in Hollywood, picturing a real person not a symbol, a stereotype, a rhetorical figure, fearing what might happen to her. *We're on the good side with y'all*. A sudden solidarity. Suddenly the speaker identifies an occasion to address a subject she believes she should address. She spots an opportunity, on the horizon of this moment, to say something she means. With little invitation she assumes common values; she begins the commonality she already believes in.

That her trust in an audience may be misplaced— that her speech may be refused, denied, punished— may or may not come as a shock.

Barbara Kopple and Cecilia Peck's 2006 documentary *Shut Up and Sing* follows this 2003 incident and its aftermath in the Chicks' lives and professional and cultural status. (Like many good smaller films, let's note, it was distributed by the Weinstein Company.) The filmmakers travel with the band, sit in as they make their next album; the scenes are intimate. We watch as these three women work through this upheaval, the national target and PR disaster they suddenly are. One of them incited it but they see it as belonging to all of them because she belongs to them and they to her. Onscreen they consider possibilities, strategies, their responsibilities to everyone they employ, the fallout and what they think it means about the musical scene they've belonged to their whole adult lives. They weigh options for tours and albums and public appearances, they swear and joke around, they meet with a new producer, write songs, have babies. *Trust in the figuring-it-out-after*, as one of my most loved friends used to say. At some point Maines made a public apology. Later she took the apology back.

∘

Off script, people say. *She went off script.* Clips circulate, get memed. We like the feel of these moments: jarred order, spectacle, vicarious freedom, recognition, resistance to powers-that-be. It feels good to see someone successful, onscreen, seeming suddenly more real, less predictable. Maybe they seem like traitors or fools, sloppy or slutty or naive. Maybe they seem more elite when they break from the script that defines the elite.

But meme-ification smooths away the jagged edges, the risk. Reception can assimilate a disruption back into the order it ruptured: disruption as another mode of assent.

You say something you think you believe in a form that's at hand. You find out if this is what you mean by saying it and seeing what happens. You trust the form you have because it's the form you have.

∘

"I hate the way they portray us in the media," rapper and producer Kanye West says in the midst of a telethon raising money after Hurricane Katrina. It's

September 2005, about a week after the hurricane devastated New Orleans. The actor and comedian Mike Myers is beside West onscreen. Myers appears to be reading fluidly from a teleprompter in order to urge donations. To anyone following the news it was clear that the government response was disturbingly slow and inadequate. When West starts speaking, he's clearly not reading. "If you see a Black family," he says, meaning in media coverage of the hurricane's survivors, "it says they're looting. If you see a white family, it says they're looking for food. And you know since it's been five days that's because most of the people are Black. And even for me to complain about it, I would be a hypocrite because I turn away from the TV because it's too hard to watch. I've even been shopping before giving a donation. So now I'm calling my business manager to see what's the biggest amount I can give, and just to imagine if I was down there, and those are my people down there […] The way America is set up to help the poor, the Black people, the less well-off, as slow as possible. I mean, Red Cross is doing everything they can. We already realize a lot of the people that could help are at war now, fighting another way, and they've given them permission to go down and shoot us." (On a TV screen behind him, helicopters move through sky, over water.)

Beside him, Myers is self-possessed but not at ease. He keeps looking over at West then back at, we assume, the teleprompter West is ignoring, moving his head as if considering nodding, but not actually nodding until the phrase *Red Cross is doing everything they can*. When

West pauses, Myers gravely reads a couple sentences, concluding, "The destruction of the spirit of the people of southern Louisiana and Mississippi may end up being the most tragic loss of all."

West says: "George Bush doesn't care about Black people."

By the time he says this line—instantly famous— he has described the violently racist complicity connecting media and American empire, and predicted the private military contractors who would soon arrive in New Orleans. In Bush's memoir, years later, he called West's comment—this "suggestion that I was a racist"—an "all-time low" of his presidency. Not the hurricane, the fate of the city and its people, its warning of climate crisis to come; not the Iraq War, which Bush chose to start then never seemed to care about. The all-time low was a suggestion that he wasn't one of the good white people. West was addressing an issue of urgent public concern, voicing with personal passion a complex social critique. Bush misunderstands this as personal, thinks it's about him. He never gets that people in New Orleans are as real as he is, that they matter to people like he matters to himself.

°

A successful "political" artist is relevant, but palatable. Not excessive; calibrated. Make a bold political statement your audience is ready to hear. Don't alienate or confuse. Criticize your fans' political opponents, not your fans. Represent them (politically, morally, aesthetically) to themselves. We should like what we see.

Many of the Chicks' fans—and definitely many industry bosses—saw them as unpatriotic, disrespecting the troops. When the band's political beliefs abruptly, publicly, departed from expectations, that was felt as a betrayal, as if they were backstabbing those who had ever allowed them success, those whose money their success was made from. Worse, weren't they disdaining their fans, siding with blue-state elitists and Europeans who looked down on red-state country-music lovers? Of course Natalie Maines may have thought she was representing only herself (in her case, three people), or those out there she rightly thought might agree. Expectations of representation aren't matters of personal choice.

The Chicks changed their name amid the Black Lives Matter protests of 2020. That spring police publicly killed George Floyd on the streets of Minneapolis, and for months protests multiplied nationwide. The name *Dixie Chicks* existed before Maines even joined the band, chosen in 1989, "we were literally teenagers when we picked that stupid name," Martie Maguire told the *New York Times*, saying "we wanted to change it years and years and years ago." (The name comes from the canonical album *Dixie Chicken* by Little Feat.) But a band name belongs to its record company, too, we have to assume. Emily Strayer—Maguire's sister,

the third bandmate—said that on social media that
year she'd seen the Confederate flag called "the Dixie
Swastika." Then the change had to be made. I was a
teenager in the deeply segregated northern state of
Connecticut, the Chicks' hit 1998 album *Wide Open
Spaces* playing in a friend's car as she gave me rides
home from track practice. Around this same time a
Connecticut Supreme Court ruling demanded school
desegregation and racial equity in public schools in
our state. As a teen I thought this victory would mean
instant change, but everything took decades, and
where I was nothing happened. The band's adjective
Dixie made my teen self uncomfortable, smacked to
my ears of Southern racism. I didn't know how the
word would be heard in the South—could it have
transcended its racist origins, could it just mean
something generally Southern, even inclusive, now?
Even from my white child's perspective that seemed
unlikely. But the discomfort must have been minor
then, for me and the Chicks. Like a blue-stater, back
then I thought where I lived must be better—more
equal, less racist—than places where words like *Dixie*
got used. Even though every day I saw evidence
otherwise. The school I attended: over 90 percent
white. Drive around and you'll see the Confederate
flag flying deep in our Yankee woods.

○

There are ways to see without seeing too much—keep
assimilating—to hear without letting yourself listen.
You sing the song, read the teleprompter, get your

grades, teach the class, hands on the wheel, wheels on the road. Even if you're not going where you meant to go.

°

Harvey Weinstein was no lone wolf. Once people started talking, started looking, they didn't stop. Weinstein, Epstein, Cosby, Lauer… Accusations—of sexual harassment, gender-based bias, misconduct, and in the worst cases assault and rape—broke through scenes and industries, through social media communities, through the realms of American publishing and literature to which I belong.

Some men lost their jobs and status; some didn't.

I kept waiting—I felt like I was waiting—for another stage to this conversation. Whatever I thought it would be, it didn't happen, not yet, not on the same scale. What should happen *after* any accusation is taken up, carried forth, after the moment of individual punishment? What should justice look or feel like in the long-term? When would this movement truly include poor and working-class people? How would prevention work? Instead we moved from climax to climax. Media established a pattern for accusations to play out.

(Even when some incidents, troublingly, didn't seem to fit the pattern. Some accusations got uncomfortably gray, seemed more like interpersonal conflict than offense. And then some—like the vague allegations against progressive politician Alex Morse, a young gay man running for Congress—proved to be entirely invented, in Morse's case weaponized by a powerful political opponent and designed to appeal to fans of old-fashioned homophobia. Morse was vindicated too late for the election, proof that this cynical tactic could work.)

Media coverage of the abusive behavior of prominent men focused on sex, not power. This long moment of reckoning confirmed how much people want to think of gender relations, and of women, in terms of sex, not power—intimacy and the domestic, not public life and social structure. Phrases like *sexual harassment* come from and mainly belong to the workplace and to public places, like the walk to work. But for the most part, narratives about sexual harassment and misconduct in work settings didn't emphasize its effects on workers *as workers*, even when it was clear this was part of the abuser's logic. Violations were narrated in emotional terms, matters of personal trauma and vulnerability, injustice as crime against an individual—yet these were also crimes against us all, against fairness, against the just distribution of wealth and power. The fact that both a main cause and effect of these violations was to keep women subordinate and block them from positions of authority was noted but went underemphasized. The comedian Louis C.K., for example, seemed to choose to sexually harass women comedians whose work he liked, potential rivals, as he himself noted when eventually backed into confessing ("I admired their work"). With each instant of harassment, he discouraged a skilled woman from continuing in the field in which he was currently dominant. As soon as he messed with them (he made fellow comedians who were women watch or listen to him masturbate), he set the terms: they either had to accept this sexual relationship with him that they'd been forced into, in a professional setting; or if they spoke out against this treatment and criticized him, he and his manager would smear them, make them seem unreliable, unstable, close all the doors that mattered. It's easy to make a woman seem crazy when she's saying something so disruptive, so scandalous: that someone you like (and maybe have invested in) committed a sexual assault.

If the problem is not just sex but power—who has it, who doesn't, and why—if the problem is not just individual but collective, that would demand much greater change than locking up a few monsters and banning more bad behavior, policing the workplace better, newer better cops, keeping everyone very equally fire-able and disposable, in the name of progress.

o

In those years, eyes on the internet, we talked about the crazy women, the truthtellers. I found that Courtney Love video, watched it again. From the YouTube stats, others were doing the same. Horrifying stories of Weinstein filled pages and screens. He'd gone to such lengths—hiring former Mossad agents, for example, to assume disguises in which to talk to his victims and learn what they were willing to say—to suppress accounts of his wrongdoing, isolate the women who'd spoken out against him, try to ensure they were seen as pariahs, unstable, unreliable. Somehow I thought the force of Love's redemption—the redemption of women like her, their purposeful, altruistic misbehavior—would change how she was thought of, how she was talked about, would elevate her in the eyes of some audience I never specified. Even though I knew the whole incident was minor, barely part of the story of this man's crimes, barely part of Love's own story. But I believed it mattered. I thought of Sinéad O'Connor. How in 1992, as you may know, it's very well known, she tore up a photograph of Pope John Paul II during her performance as the musical guest on *Saturday Night Live*. For years that was kind of all I knew about this act (in '92, I was 11). Then another phrase got attached to it: *to protest child abuse in the Catholic Church*. She'd sung, a cappella, Bob Marley's song "War," a protest of racism and colonialism, lyrics based on a speech Haile Selassie gave to the UN in 1963. But she altered the lyrics to place an emphasis on child abuse. In the US, the *Boston Globe*'s major stories on child abuse in the Catholic Church would start appearing in 2002, ten years after O'Connor's protest: when, as she reached the song's concluding lines, which speak of "the victory of good over evil," she held up the Pope's image, obscuring her own face, then tore it in half, looking right into the camera as she tore the photo again and tossed it at the floor, saying simply, "fight the real enemy" (after which, in absolute silence, standing amid an arrangement of lit white candles, she removed her earpieces). In my youth O'Connor was talked about like she was crazy, like she was kind of cool and interesting, kind of laughable. Her '92 stunt was described as a stunt, something big and weird someone did, something shocking, like the attention and not the content was the point. A curiosity. Among teens she wasn't necessarily hated, as she was by pundits and commentators at the time, but she wasn't respected, she wasn't treated like an authority on the subject she'd chosen, in a big way, to address.

So what happens if you listen?

◦

Before it's a prophecy, it's just something people know and more powerful people don't want to have to admit. These truths aren't esoteric. Common knowledge. The elite setting of the media tends to treat such statements (Love's, Maines's, West's, O'Connor's) as spectacle more than as knowledge shared. None of this is an exposure, not really; the truth was, as the cliché affirms, hidden in plain sight. George W. Bush cares more about white people than Black people, than Muslims, Arabs, go on—of course. His lifelong actions are the proof. Plenty of Texans, plenty of country music fans, plenty of women, didn't support the Iraq War (though they and their kids had to suffer and die in it). Weinstein's predation was an open secret. Child abuse in the Catholic Church was suffered and known by tens of thousands. Sexual harassment and inequity in the workplace, well-known from McDonald's and Walmart to NBC, CBS, Hollywood, the White House. In one act of saying, common knowledge can get empowered. But this requires new listening. This instance of speech is commonplace in content, yet exceptional in form and in context, and therein lies its courage.

∘

Maybe we listen best when we feel someone has trusted us—us especially—to listen.

∘

In college a friend was dating my boyfriend's roommate, on the other side of the wall. All us girlfriends of that room group (a college dorm concept) sort of banded together. My friend was in the same situation as I was, but worse, and she was better at it. Our boyfriends had musical taste and we didn't. Her boyfriend was, in her view, a musical snob, and she liked what she liked, pop music and the women singer-songwriters of our day. I usually felt ashamed, a bit inferior, a little bored, insecure, when good or important music was played that I didn't enjoy, when I didn't know the group or even the genre, the basic category, everyone was talking about, when people made fun of something I basically liked. My friend was neither bored nor insecure. At a little family party for her graduation she watched as her boyfriend caught the background music playing—the expression on his face. She howled with laughter. I knew you'd hate it, she said, then said to the rest of us: guys, this is a CD called *Jazz for When You're in Love*. Isn't it great?

On a car trip sometime to somewhere she popped in a Sinéad O'Connor CD. He hates it, she said, nodding to her boyfriend in the passenger seat (I was in the back), he might have briefly discreetly groaned—but don't you think, she said to me, that she's really good? Isn't she good? I agreed that Sinéad was really good, not because I'd ever thought about it before or knew what I thought then, but because my friend was good, I wanted to be on her side, I couldn't tell if I liked the music or not, probably because I couldn't tell if I should.

○

In the autumn of the pandemic, I walked around the neighborhood listening to audiobooks, through old headphones that fit badly in my very pierced ears. This book was a massive beautiful sociological study of 1,000 American women who'd sought abortions up to or beyond the threshold of the gestational limit— this isn't one limit, but many; it varies by clinic, by state. (And not to falsely assume that everyone seeking abortion care is a woman. In this study the pregnant people enrolled all identified as women.) These women had either received the abortion they'd wanted or been turned away—the book is titled *The Turnaway*

Study. Interviews conducted over five years (ending in 2015) tracked what happened with that pregnancy and/or child, with the next pregnancy, with school and employment, personal and family finances, plans for the future, relationships and partnerships, other children in the family, her health (two women in the study later died in childbirth), health insurance (one woman who learned she was pregnant five months in, too late, was consoled by the fact that she could now, because pregnant, get Medicaid and get her teeth fixed, which would help her finally get a good job). The study was covered widely in the news, in congressional hearings, perhaps you glimpsed it, since it disproved persistent fears about abortion. There's little regret afterward and no adverse effects on mental or physical health. "95% of women consistently felt abortion was the right decision for them over the course of the study." In the book, chapters discussing the study's findings are interspersed with long personal narratives, monologues shaped from the in-depth interviews conducted over years. What struck me as I walked in large circles around my own house—the pleasant residential inner-ring suburb of Cleveland Heights, Ohio, just then flush with signs stating *Black Lives Matter* and opposing Donald Trump, who was about to win the state of Ohio for a second time—was the correspondence between the social science and this personal narration. Not just on one point or another but overall. Overall the reasons people gave for why they'd wanted an abortion—in their own language when attentively asked—these reasons anticipated what the study would prove, the realities for which it would provide evidence. People's economic situation and outlook, relationships, educational progress, plans, family dynamics, personal health—all tend to be affected by an unplanned pregnancy in just the ways these women expected. We know our own lives, expertly. We know the forces acting on us. What I'm saying is simple but the proof felt weighty. Every day we are reasoning, intimately and soundly. These women were all highly reasonable. Science undertook years of work to confirm how right they were. This reasoning is personal but comprehends the social and cultural and political and economic. This book about abortion was also about the success of everyday acts of thinking.

2. I'm sorry

Even in the midst of the pandemic, the pandemic felt far away. Even as it wholly changed our daily lives. The news reported thousands then millions of deaths. The word *unprecedented* appeared in so many emails, including mine. I was one of those workers who were sent home, locked down, work gone remote, all email and online meetings, confined day and night to one's apartment or home, one's place of living. The workers in this category were mostly middle-class, or richer, and disproportionately white. Those still on the job, "in person," at wildly greater risk of illness and death, were mostly working class, and disproportionately African American and people of color.

Maybe because I've rarely felt in control of my health, I was less afraid for myself. My futile anxiety was for my students, for all those losing jobs, losing family members, for the American lack of social infrastructure whose brutality we were witnessing. I wanted to "socially distance" because I wanted to do the right thing; naively I didn't really fear, for me personally, the virus. So, I felt, I should be out there working. Since it would bother me less; since I'd be happy to do it. But that's not how things work. When crisis arrives, it comes to you where you are. You don't suddenly get to switch, for example, your job, your socioeconomic status, for this next dramatic act. No matter your feelings.

I thought of that phrase *news from elsewhere*: an

everyday phrase I'd long taken as goad and site of confrontation. If you sit near the center of an empire, a moral task is to make *elsewhere* feel near, to make clear the connections between what we do here and what is done to people there. The pandemic was *here*; the US was a country besieged and badly struggling, the virus overwhelming our hospitals and communities. Every day our newly constrained routines were a sacrifice on behalf of others, a practice acknowledging interdependence and our human, immune closeness. Yet I felt more elsewhere than ever. The news was near—was right here—yet I felt far.

That spring American institutions began to publicly speak the language of illness, of disability—a language usually marginalized. Universities made statements about how students might get sick and miss class, faculty might get sick and miss their teaching, their work. There'd long been some mechanisms (well, not really when I was in college) for acknowledging students as people in vulnerable bodies—an Office of Disability Services; instances of illness and missed class to navigate with compassion—but less so for teachers, for workers. In March, as covid was beginning its big sweep across the US, I got sick. A little flu, probably. Maybe covid. I doubt I'll ever know, doubt it matters. How it mattered was this: I sent a couple emails noting I was ill and would be back in touch soon, a couple emails upon recovery apologizing for delay, *I've been sick.* People would receive these notes with warmth and sympathy, I realized, with accommodation, even solidarity. Right now illness was something we were all in together.

(Online I read speculation that when this time was over, people wouldn't speak of it. We'd all agree to bury it, this time of vulnerability and suffering.)

Like many with chronic illness, I know it as isolating and differentiating. Paradoxically common, this experience of isolation. Illness sets you apart, marks you. As less capable, less present, weaker, weirder, needier... When I'm late with something because of my illness I tend to feel panicked, ashamed. In my thirties I cultivated the habit of telling people when I'm sick, telling people that I have an illness. I think I believe this is useful advocacy and transparency. Yet it's rarely felt liberating. And ironically I can only try this approach because my health has improved enough, since its worst point, that I now have a job, have a reason to email anyone, there are people who include me in their work and expect things of me. If you're sick enough you're no longer late because you no longer make plans—the world of obligations, responsibilities, and expectations has receded from you, or you from it. When I mention my illness, say something about being sick, in some work email, I tend to feel exposed, burdensome, not free. It's uncomfortable to bring my body into this email. I fear my name will start to have a sort of asterisk beside it: unavailable, unreliable, complicated, "messy." If a friend or student or stranger spoke to me of living with a chronic illness, I would argue they should never feel what I just described feeling. It is immoral to shame anyone for their basic mortality, the basic facts and risks of our embodied lives. But I feel that shame, that stigma. Shame has this power: you'd contest it for others, yet feel it all the more yourself. They shouldn't feel this, but you should—you deserve this, only and especially you.

But in these months—spring 2020—telling someone you had covid-19 didn't come with this familiar shame. (Later it would; later people would judge you for not being "safe" enough: the cruel purity judgments around contagion.) In that environment I felt a little free—writing *I seem to have the flu*, needing to delay something for a day or two, it's fine. I felt I'd be received with care. It was a little liberation that angered me. Why couldn't I always feel that care?

Yet—I've just told you—the shame I felt was *mine*. Was I its origin and its destination, shame's perpetrator and victim? Was care always present, always possible, and I just couldn't recognize it? Was I the one excluding myself?

°

In another summer I was listening to an audiobook of Hannah Arendt's *The Life of the Mind*. That was hard. I could not get distracted by flowering bushes or pinwheels the neighbor kids had made from old cans of my favorite beer. In one passage Arendt describes how what is most intimate and specific and necessary to us as individuals is also least identifiable, most interchangeable with others. Meaning, for example (this is her example), our internal organs. My heart, my lungs—I couldn't pick them out of a lineup.

This is the problem of the symptom. The category of the symptom extracts your personal experiences and packages them with a label that established regimes of knowledge can recognize. This can be a relief, a means toward help. You're not alone in this, this makes sense to someone, means something they can act on. The irritating pain in your shoulder indicates a tumor in your liver, which we will now shrink and remove. Your desire to weigh less than 90 pounds is not your own dreamed-up madness, it's a problem people have, a disorder that can end. These episodes of pain and weakness, this disability you know so thoroughly, all this can be named. The name is a path toward treatment, inclusion in a pattern, something you can expect, something you share with others, a means to decrease the chaos of your experience. The symptom attaches you to a description, makes of your mystery and interiority (no one else can feel your headache, your shoulder pain) something that can be known and changed. This process affirms you. The symptom is not you. It is a disease you are experiencing. The symptom belongs to something outside you, the disease, a pattern that isn't personal. (If you die of the disease, after all, it's you who dies. The disease goes on.)

But the symptom feels like you. You are feeling it. It shapes your hours and days; it forms your ways of being. At times it dominates what you know as yourself and how you know anything. It defines you because it is something you can't control about yourself. It's you happening to yourself. The symptoms I am thinking of are those of the mind. Medical discourse might say *brain*, but brain isn't what you feel. I'd been experiencing these symptoms more frequently, for years, and in the year of the pandemic I tried to speak of them, the symptoms, which were me. Since adolescence I'd had neurological issues. Episodic, seemingly not progressive. Atypical migraine, they eventually said. Complex migraine. Migraine can be severely debilitating, debilitatingly severe, but that's not what the name first suggests. Rather, an inconvenience, pain for no purpose and reason to which women (mostly women), stressed, succumb. The actor Ben Affleck once went to the ER for a migraine (it happens, it's common) and was mocked online. Maybe migraine is not seen as a disability but a problem, something people should deal with, suck it up. Something fair enough, if disability is often called *unfair*. There's a line, ill-defined, something that shapes our expectations of one another, the depth and nature of our care.

Doctors once directed me to a website, where other doctors had written: "People with [disease name] are in a difficult position in a world where we still classify things in terms of physical and mental illnesses, even though this makes very little sense when one is talking about the brain."

o

The symptoms I hate most could be called an affliction of shame. It's not just that I feel shame for experiencing these symptoms. The symptoms are an incarnation of shame. My migraines—these episodes—whatever they are—take, thousands of times in my life, a familiar form. Muscle weakness, severe fatigue, difficulty walking, cognitive difficulty or "brain fog," head and face pain, muscle spasms, nightmares. It used to be that a few times a year, a deeper depression—I would say despair—arrived in the midst of an episode. Like a weight at the center suddenly plummeting. I used to think I was feeling despair because I was so often sick. Not sure what kind of life would be possible with this much illness. Then I thought the despair was simply another further form of the illness—the same illness extending its range of symptoms. Does it matter which of those theories is true? I sit on the floor unable to stop crying. It seems to have little to do with me. At some point I came to understand that this crying *has almost nothing to do with me*, with the person I know as myself. It's happening to me. My thoughts circle furiously. My mind finds an interpersonal incident—a professional difficulty, awkward interaction, strained relationship—and drags it around a cruel and furious circle, narrating and narrating and narrating, for hours. An unending circling narrating jabbering hopeless thinking that I recognize from daily life, but amplified. Escalating into a feeling of ruin. Ruin has entered my life, like a flaw or rot, and now it's there, inherent, forever.

These days used to happen a few times a year, always while I was having my usual neurological symptoms, which is why I understood them as a worse aspect of this same disease. Then they got more frequent. A few days like this a month. And so, right before the pandemic, I began seeking new medical care, though over two decades I'd intermittently given up on the promise of treatment, having tried every drug in the book, having dutifully auditioned for one diagnosis too many. Sometimes I would point out to professionals that—since most neurological medication has significant side effects, and seeking medical care in the US, through our miserable insurance system, is time-consuming and very expensive—this decades-long process of trying a few dozen medications had harmed me far more than it had ever helped.

During these dark episodes, as I sometimes call them, I suffer more when I know I am witnessed. If I know myself as someone other people have to live with. If I know my life can ruin theirs too. I don't want to talk to anyone. I don't want to be seen. On my own, I put on some TV. If someone—my husband—comes to check on me, I don't want it, I can't bear it. Don't see me. I'll say to him everything I feel, which is *I'm sorry*
I'm sorry
I'm sorry
I'm sorry
I'm sorry
I'm sorry
I'm sorry
I'm sorry

I'm sorry
I'm sorry
I'm sorry
I'm sorry
I'm sorry
I'm sorry
I'm sorry
I'm sorry
I'm sorry
I'm sorry
I'm sorry
I'm sorry
I'm sorry

I'm sorry
I'm sorry
I'm sorry
I'm sorry
I'm sorry
I'm sorry
I'm sorry
I'm sorry
I'm sorry
I'm sorry
I'm sorry
I'm sorry
I'm sorry
I'm sorry

○

Please stop apologizing

o

During the pandemic so much programming was online, accessible to people with chronic illnesses and disabilities, as never before. In lockdown, those of us working from home often missed working in person, but before lockdown, many of us had wanted to work from home more often and had not been permitted. Many had wanted more online ("remote") options and programming, and those didn't exist. About a year into the pandemic, we suspected that much of remote or hybrid remote/in person life would be here to stay. We'll have more flexibility now, people reflected, more online meetings that don't need to be in person, more accommodation, less commuting. Yet, a friend added, this might be the end of sick days. From the bosses' perspective, if you can work from home, why would you ever need—do you *really* need—a day off?

o

I was getting tired. There's no point in putting it like that. *I'm getting tired. I feel worn out.* You can't take a break from chronic illness. You can point out how useful a break would be. You can observe that you never have, not really, a vacation, because you often get sick as soon as there's a break in work (common pattern), and because you are sick so often you are usually a little behind in every kind of obligation, so any break becomes a chance to catch up. But I was starting to say things like, *it's hard to come back*. I meant from the despair days, which were becoming more frequent. It feels like, I said to a friend, when you finally feel better, when the spell of illness breaks, after four or five or eight days, you wake back up into your life and you're just running flat out. The bus of your life is like three blocks away and you have to catch it. You have to make it seem like you were on it, you were right there, the whole time. It didn't, of course, feel like that. Not cute like that. Like the phrase *brain fog*, which sounds misty, like weather that will burn off into sun, not like a profound struggle to be yourself, to use language, to think, to understand. *No point getting tired if you can't rest*, I thought sometimes. I don't think this thought helped.

○

If it's sudden, you might scream. Pain's arrival. You are suddenly sitting on the kitchen floor. Immediately you need to be somewhere else. In bed, in the dark, far away. It's hard to get there. The kitchen is public. Though only four of you live here. You think of your illness as semi-private, though it must also be public. During a year of pandemic lockdown, it's strange to say you spend days of illness *confined*. Everyone is confined. Yet when you're well, there's a house, a neighborhood, a job, meetings with others online. When sick, there's a bedroom and long dark hours. When illness lifts a bit in the evenings, you come down to dinner. Your three housemates (husband, two friends) are there, they've cooked, they're chatting, a baseball game may be playing spectrally, projected on the wall. You belong to a world.

Once, in the kitchen, you screamed. Your housemate rushed to the stairs. You could hear his quick footsteps. He must, then, have heard you sobbing, heard the voice of your husband, and understood. Understood illness so well he would never have mentioned it. A harsh scream through the daylit house, this sudden interior violence, accepted like anything, with care. Later you apologized to him for the disturbance, an apology no one needed and which was only a way to thank the house for its everyday mercy.

Through lockdown there are the four of you, in this capacious Cleveland house with its grab-bag furniture. You've often lived like this—rarely with just your husband or partner, often with others, in different combinations, in put-together places. It's better than being just a couple—for each person, there is more than one person around, for help and company and courtesy, to run a little errand, to chat about a frustration. During the pandemic you feel some pride in, or just gratitude for, this habit of living—when the music of everyday life stopped, here you were, together, during this time of mass isolation and distance.

o

In 2013 Sinéad O'Connor began a public correspondence—a series of open letters and social media posts, exchanged—with the pop singer Miley Cyrus. Cyrus had cited O'Connor's 1990 music video "Nothing Compares 2 U" (O'Connor's huge hit, cover

of a Prince song) in her new single "Wrecking Ball."
She'd praised this artist of a previous generation,
26 years her senior; her close-cut hair resembled
O'Connor's famously shaved head, though Cyrus's
hair was styled and bleached where O'Connor's
was minimal, blunt. (The story goes that O'Connor
shaved her head early on so she couldn't get treated
like the pretty girl.)

In O'Connor's video, now canonical, scenes of the
singer clad in a black cloak, neck to ankle, walking
through what looks like a manor garden, stone
architecture and statuary, trees and moss (it's a
cemetery, Père Lachaise), are interspersed with
close-ups against a dark background, her face filling
the screen, wide gray-green eyes, visible vulnerable
emotion. Four minutes into the song you see tears
form in her eyes. A single tear descends each cheek.
Apocryphally the crying wasn't performed, was
unplanned, O'Connor says she was thinking just
then—at that point in the song—of her mother, who
had passed away a few years before, and who had
abused her when she was a child.

Cyrus's 2013 video begins with an obviously similar
close-up. She is already crying: instant citation,
pastiche. I guess Cyrus's team wanted to evoke
something classic, *iconic*. Impatient commodification:
just cut to the part people liked best (the memorable
off-script moment).

The "Wrecking Ball" video was popular and

"controversial" because Cyrus's performance—in an abstracted industrial-ish gray structure that a wrecking ball picturesquely smashes through, while in the foreground Cyrus wields a sledgehammer, cuddling it, swinging it—was forthrightly sexual. She rides the wrecking ball suggestively, she licks the sledgehammer. She's a good singer but the video is silly. You're left to interpret her overtures to this construction equipment as expressions of her availability to the absent lover the song addresses, this lover the singer has wronged, or loved too intensely to last. Like, *I will love you like I love this sledgehammer I'm licking*. That's funny. But she's crying? This blend of camp and borrowed, referential emotional sincerity is a dead-end. The performance uses sexual energy to try to get at something real, something raw, but sexuality—especially when performed to a sledgehammer, by someone who seems like they've never used a sledgehammer, on what is obviously an expensive video set, singing lyrics so general there's no way to say what inspired anyone to write them, other than their desire to write a pop song—doesn't necessarily feel real, or raw, or authentic, like you mean it, like it was your idea.

O'Connor's first letter offered Cyrus professional advice on being a woman in their industry, warning her against those who would exploit her sexuality for their own profit. "The music business doesn't give a shit about you, or any of us," she wrote:

> They will prostitute you for all you
> are worth, and cleverly make you

think its what YOU wanted … and when you end up in rehab as a result of being prostituted, 'they' will be sunning themselves on their yachts in Antigua, which they bought by selling your body and you will find yourself very alone. […]

Don't think for a moment that any of them give a flying fuck about you. They're there for the money… we're there for the music. It has always been that way and will always be that way. […]

Women are to be valued for so much more than their sexuality. We aren't merely objects of desire. I would be encouraging you to send healthier messages to your peers … that they and you are worth more than what is currently going on in your career. Kindly fire any motherfucker who hasn't expressed alarm, because they don't care about you.

The letter was called condescending and too maternal—O'Connor says she wrote it "in a spirit of motherliness and with love"—but you couldn't say the advice was unsolicited, since Cyrus had cited her colleague multiple times. The correspondence took off; media called it a *feud*. What was remarkable was how sincere O'Connor always seemed.

Sincerity may be a false idol. Some of the most destructive things ever said to me or in my presence were defended by their speaker as *sincere*, as if this quality absolved the speaker of consequences, granted speech a sacred status. Yet beyond sincerity lies trust. Beyond what might be heard as condescension, O'Connor seemed to believe that Cyrus would be interested to hear from her, that because they have a lot in common they naturally would want to talk. Dialogue, in mutual respect, shared love of their shared art, women working in a patriarchal field. O'Connor's language can be harshly critical. But she seems to trust that conversation is possible and valuable. Cyrus's responses provide no evidence that she wants this dialogue or any relationship at all with the other singer. (When asked by a reporter if the two singers might "kiss and make up," Cyrus replies flippantly, on-brand, "I don't know. Are we supposed to kiss?")

If a woman challenges you, you can always call her crazy. Cyrus then shared a series of social media posts O'Connor had made two years before, in which she described herself as experiencing a mental health crisis and openly sought recommendations for a local psychiatrist. Cyrus prefaced the post with a short mocking note comparing O'Connor to a young woman actor whose struggles with mental illness were the subject of recent media feeding. In reply, O'Connor is forceful in her account of how harmful such actions are toward those with mental illness, who should not be ashamed of—should not be shamed for—their existence or their need for medical care. That kind of shame, she notes, is a cause of suicide. She emphasizes that she's a mother of four and can't afford to be considered "unemployable." (That Cyrus didn't note that these posts were several years old, dug up from the past, is one of O'Connor's main complaints.) Curiously, Cyrus could use O'Connor's own past public words as a weapon to incite new shame. Shame works this way: to make someone bear witness to herself at the height of her suffering. To make them and us see it again, without mercy. Watching this feud play out, we onlookers feel shame, too, at Cyrus—that she's one of us and that we are, despite ourselves, looking on at her cruelty.

In her discussions of experiencing mental illness O'Connor tends to describe herself as "one of millions" (as she says in another video), a public representative who has, as she notes, more resources than most. Evidently she trusts that she can speak in a way that benefits others. In this case she keeps talking to her colleague, not altering her approach even when it's not working. This could be read as optimistic, desperate, naïve, blinkered, inspiring. She holds the door open. She seems to think that at any moment Cyrus might decide to walk through it, sit on a stool in the kitchen and hash things out. That this never happens—never even one sign it might—doesn't seem to alter her faith.

o

When I witness faith like this, I feel embarrassed. A thought occurs to me like, *But don't you know how things are?* Something in me wants the status quo acknowledged. This, of course, becomes a means to defend it. *Of course people with mental illness are stigmatized,* I seem to be thinking, *of course they—we—get called crazy, it's always been this way.* I don't like or want this line of thought, it just happens. It's there in me, patrolling the borders along which society discriminates, asking questions like, *well, what did you expect?*

How can they be surprised, this thought goes, *That's how things are. That's just how things are.*

o

In the summer of 2020, articles and books were featured and discussed with new intensity throughout the media: how to practice anti-racism; how to do diversity work. These discussions were mostly directed at white people like me, in part because most media centers white audiences, and in part because white people have long had the least incentive to do this work and lack knowledge and motivation. Phrases like *systemic racism*, *white supremacy*, and *structural bias* became more prominent—useful tools in directing people's attention away from what we had or hadn't done or thought personally, and toward the legacies of history and inequities of institutions we might not have yet recognized.

At the same time, the actions and solutions discussed, at least in mainstream media, focused on the individual. This seemed convenient for institutions, which could receive praise for purging individual employees, or blandly posting social media messages of solidarity and announcing some new internship programs, rather than being forced to redistribute wealth and power. This type of response sometimes seemed cynical, like it was about visibility and the short attention span of social media, how to satisfy short-term appetites. Yet it also might reflect a profound desire to do something, here and now. Which took form as posting, having one immediate paragraph of language you could share, a donation made, a concrete action taken and noted—even if on reflection this might not seem sufficient, or even that effective a choice.

We needed and wanted to consider systems, but we had so much more language for individuals.

A friend and I were discussing strategies for workplaces like ours. Diversity work. What would make a difference there, where we spent our days and labor? We landed on the sort of hypothetical you use to think something through. The details don't matter. We arrived into a question about actions vs. thoughts. If we want to change our own and others' actions, change how individual actions contribute to and comprise a collective endeavor, when should we focus on action vs. on worldview, the thinking that drives how people act? The strategy we'd come up with, our little example, focused on action: encouraging people to act certain ways and not other ways. OK, we thought, would that work? When you are steered toward certain forms of action, don't you start to think in their terms? If your daily labor is structured to include diversity work, you may come to see how it benefits you, too, or *is* you, and your thinking will change, will start to include and value actions like this. Maybe.

I found myself saying to my friend: thoughts don't really matter. Thoughts aren't that personal. Racist thoughts, for example, are evil, but they can't be that personal because they're all so similar. Stereotypical thinking is the same everywhere, pouring tiresomely out of people's mouths at any time, manifesting in their actions with an exhausting horrifying predictability. Whenever I've noticed myself thinking a stereotype (do I always notice?), it has felt like I was *reproducing* something, like I could see how I'd just thought a stereotype that exists in endless forms outside me, from children's books to high-school bus chatter to the rhetoric of politicians and commentators that echoes through the news. The effects of this hateful thinking are personal, but its cause seems more collective than individual. And since people regularly are able to think one thing and hypocritically do something opposing, thoughts can't finally determine actions. I was thinking aloud to my friend more honestly, on this subject of thinking, than I usually would. So many thoughts, I heard myself saying, that I've ever thought I didn't even want to think. I mean, a lot of thoughts that are, I guess, "mine" feel like they're happening to me. They're not mine, I would never choose them, I don't like them at all.

°

So, if you can—if you are able, if someone helps, if we hear each other cry out, if we may learn and recognize and respond—if you ever can, you get free.

3. You need me to see it

In the fall of the year of the pandemic my hands stopped working. This was new. When I tried to use my hands they were sluggish and weak. One day they curled in on themselves and stayed that way, like claws, cold and purpling. I was scared. I read for hours online about Parkinson's. It wasn't. My hands got better; they're better right now.

The weakness, I learned, was functional. There's no underlying disease, no cause. The brain is just making a mistake and the mistake is the problem, there's no problem causing the mistake. The brain is obstructing the hands' ordinary working. Something about how everything ordinarily works has been forgotten or obscured. You can catch it in the act. The weakness isn't there when the hand moves spontaneously. Only when you choose to move it. Only when you bring your attention to it, when you do something intentionally. Apparently these are different pathways: intending to do vs. doing without thinking. I'd never heard of this problem. Here it is. When the doctor described it—noting that, in her office, I'd struggled immensely to write my name when asked, but that I had been able later, swiftly and thoughtlessly, to pick up a pencil and drop it in my bag—I realized I knew what she meant. I'd witnessed this phenomenon but I couldn't understand it; it's hard to understand something that seems like your own madness. When I tried to use my hands they were weak, limited, painful—when, for example, I reached to pick up a clean dish and put it in the cupboard. But when I did something without thinking—if someone asked me to pass them a dish and I grabbed it without thinking—everything went better. I told her: I noticed this, but I couldn't figure it out. When I'd clocked this strange phenomenon, I'd tried to recreate it. I'd taken a deep breath, calmly and casually reached for another dish. But it was, again, hard. My hands were weak again.

Yes, the doctor said, because the second time, you were bringing your attention to it. As soon as you do that, it triggers the dysfunction.

For this reason—the doctor explained—you could never really see the problem yourself. You need someone outside you to see it. You need me to see it.

The diagnostic term for this phenomenon, *functional neurological disorder*, is an update of *conversion disorder*, itself an update of *hysteria*. The diagnosis *conversion disorder* had been pinned on me and unpinned from me by various doctors in the past. The diagnosis had never been offered (not to me) as a path to treatment; rather to exclude me from other treatment, from the proper halls of neurology where malingerers were unwelcome. Conversion disorder required two problems, one which was being converted into another: psychological distress manifesting as physiological symptoms. Psychosomatic. This didn't mean, shouldn't be understood to mean (though it often was), that people were manufacturing the symptoms themselves. This all took place below the level of consciousness, beyond agency. Psychic suffering that's gone long unaddressed, unarticulated, translates itself into something more concrete and urgent: a physiological problem.

In contrast, this newly named disorder required no underlying trauma, no primary psychological issue. Many people who suffered from it seemed to have average psychological health, no depression, no indicative history of trauma. Often they had another, more severe and intractable neurological illness. This disorder was just something that could happen, like any disease, neutrally, to anyone. It meant something for you but it didn't mean anything about you.

°

That's maddening, I said, almost happily, when this new diagnosis was explained to me. To get to say something is maddening is so much nicer than thinking *I've gone mad*.

Yes, it is a very interesting disease, the doctor's fellow added, almost happily, from the corner.

°

Sometimes I try to read Twitter—where tons of journalism and cultural commentary now takes place—and I wonder: where's my old rhetorical triangle? *Text, purpose, audience.* There's barely a text. Conversations disappear. Things happen there that alter the life and reputation of a person or organization, but then you can't find them. You can't cite them, they don't exist, though their effect does (real, but always lacking evidence). Each text possesses algorithmically its own audience, which you can't know from outside, and so you can't know its purpose, what kind of performance this is, what conversation this post was responding to or wanting to incite. Everything is public but not meant for a public— either it's kept bland and commercial in order to serve nearly everyone, or it's for a specific audience that is almost always not you. "Context collapse," theorists of the internet call this. Reply threads become chains of misinterpretation, bad-faith attacks, sycophancy, conspiratorial side-taking, attention-seeking, failed reading, proliferating response that is speech without dialogue.

Does *online activism*—political engagement on social media—suppress "real world" activism? Does the existence of online activism lead to less activism rather than more? This is my fear. Of course not— counterargument—because social media is used vitally to incite and communicate about real-world protests: during the Arab Spring, during the 2020 Black Lives Matter movement. But this isn't social media's main use, hour by hour. I fear that if there is a virtual realm (Twitter, Facebook, etc.) in which you can act and be affirmed for acting (posting), there's less incentive to figure out how to act beyond that. You feel as if you've acted; others respond to you as if you've acted. In this fear, social media is a tool the powerful can use to distract you from actually doing something. Posting is just easier. Tech companies have made a playground where people can mock-fight all day. Except they're really fighting. The playground is set up, algorithmically, to encourage fights: you respond to posts mainly through affiliation or opposition. These sites are designed to encourage polarizing modes of engagement because those are powerful modes of engagement for people to experience. The site's goal is to keep you on the site, where you'll keep interacting and your attention and behavioral information will remain available for data mining, to be extracted and sold, sold, sold. If you spend all day shoving people in the virtual playground, at the end of the day you're tired, and you haven't spent one minute fighting the surveillance capitalists who made the playground and make money off every minute you're there.

That fear concerns the collective. A second fear about social media concerns the individual, and it may be worse. Let's say: a brutal injustice is occurring, widely covered by news. People in the online literary community, for example, are posting about it in solidarity. There's pressure for everyone in the community to do the same. The injustice is probably being supported at least in part, if not whole, by the US government. So there is something hopeful about so many Americans sharing their opposition to it, educating one another about it. Yet, if I myself go to post, I have a disturbed, disgusted feeling. Is this pure necropolitics? My post does not really do anything to stop the Israeli military's killing of the people of the

Gaza. Instead it feels like I am using the people of Gaza's suffering, their murder, to gain social capital for myself. To gain recognition as a good person. I am gaining a good feeling at a bargain cost—I said something, I took a moral stance, which feels good, it lets me feel less futile and powerless. But am I using others' suffering to gain affirmation and belonging? Am I seeking out a shortcut to attain the personal benefits of ethical action? Is that what this gesture mostly means and is?

Online it starts to feel like people can't tell what work is, they can't tell what anything does. If you do something—if you work hard to do something meaningful—but you don't post about it, you're kind of not doing anything. And if your post does some damage, but you didn't post that you *meant* it to do that, it kind of didn't. Sincerity in hell.

°

No surprise that Sinéad O'Connor's career suffered after the protest on *Saturday Night Live*, or in the words of the *New York Times* it "killed her career." Scandal followed, birth of a pariah—for an artist who'd been, according to *Spin*, "a star on the same level as Madonna and Prince." One week later Joe Pesci hosted *SNL* and said that if he'd been there during her performance he'd have "given her such a smack." Not the only threat of violence. She was banned from NBC. Commentary looking back on the incident notes that because major coverage of the extent of child abuse in the Catholic Church hadn't yet broken in the US, most viewers didn't understand what she was talking about. Some thought the protest was about women's rights. "In the popular cultural memory of the United States, O'Connor remains a crazy woman," in PRI's 2014 analysis.

In 2021, O'Connor publishes a memoir, and the surrounding big-media coverage is often warm and receptive, framing O'Connor as an authentic, independent, battle-weary woman artist who's been long misunderstood. Overall this doesn't feel like a redemption, twenty-nine years later. It feels like O'Connor's '92 protest, softened by time, now overlaps with the kinds of political speech desired from pop artists—though these contemporary pop political statements tend to be slicker, clearer, more calculated, and minimally harm sales. From a safe distance her long-ago lonely act can be repackaged as the new commodity.

°

Of course my perspective on social media is (like all my perspectives) American, where Donald Trump has ruled the medium, dominated the discourse. *Greatest poster of all time*, online leftists posted when Twitter banned Trump late in his presidency. Not because they were Trump supporters but just to recognize. His Tweets *were* the news. Social media was born in the US and its companies influence our government, gentrify our cities, drive our economic inequality.

Elsewhere social media may feel more like resistance to authoritarian power, realize more of its potential as grassroots tool, democratic mode. I don't know. I live here.

The scandal around O'Connor's '92 gesture was largely American, though she's Irish and was speaking in the context of Irish culture and history. Like many Americans I have to remind myself she wasn't necessarily speaking to mainstream America; the white Americans who banned her may not have comprised her main context or audience. (In fact, in her memoir she describes the *SNL* protest as emerging out of time spent with West Indian immigrants in New York, getting exposed to the Rastafari movement.) Mine is a common slippage among white Americans: appropriating and fetishizing Irish identity. For white Americans, "Irishness" can serve as a source of identity in which one's ancestors may not have been simply colonizers, arriving from Europe to America, but also victims of empire whose emigration was a means to survive brutal imperial British rule. It's a tempting alternative story in a nation born of settler colonialism and the genocide of indigenous peoples.

In an interview the day after her *SNL* appearance, O'Connor describes her action as a response to the Catholic Church's complicity in the colonization of Ireland, and colonization as a cause of child abuse. This protest was about Ireland and made possible in America. She took advantage of this live American TV show to, in her words, "create an opportunity for people, including myself, to say how they feel. […] I couldn't find any way of saying it anywhere, and there didn't seem to be any way for anyone else to say it, and so I thought, well, fuck it." In the video of this interview, just then she makes a gesture of tearing, reproducing her gesture from the night before —though then she was standing tall and looking right into the camera, at millions, whereas now she's leaning forward, elbows on her knees, looking alternately down at the floor and up at a man sitting close beside her, interviewing her, for a reggae TV show called Viddyms.

She's asked how far in advance she planned this action: "About a week."

"And you neglected to tell the producers of the show or anyone connected with the show about this?" the interviewer asks.

She smiles and says: "Yeah, 'cause I didn't—see, if it was in Ireland, there's no way they'd have let me do that, and I thought they wouldn't let me if I asked them, so I behaved accordingly."

○

Treatment for functional neurological disorder often involves physical therapy. Train the brain back into function by training the body. If your brain has troubled the function of your hands, you can start by reminding your hands how to work, which reminds the brain. You can solve a brain problem with a body solution. That's probably not the way to put it. Physical therapy has helped treat some of my functional issues remarkably well. My hands got better not long after I learned the name *functional neurological disorder* and understood the problem was no worse than that.

Yes, the doctor's fellow told me on the phone, for some people just learning what it is seems to improve the condition. It is very interesting, he said again.

4. It depends on what you mean

This October 4, 1992, interview on Viddyms is available on YouTube, unedited, including dead space for commercials and multiple takes of the intro and of a statement O'Connor reads at the end. The host, Tony Lindo, introduces her: "Those of us who listen to reggae music or who are maybe interested in the Rastafari culture know that there's some similarities between what she's been saying about the Pope and what we've been saying for a long time." Her cover of Bob Marley's "War" brought her here. Partway through the interview Lindo challenges her reggae knowledge, wants to see if she knows the genre beyond Marley. She does fine.

In the interview they sit knee to knee. O'Connor is on a large rattan chair and Lindo is perched on a folding chair close by, so they need just his microphone, which he tilts cozily toward her when she speaks. The pair look like they're wedged in a corner; there may be some brooms leaning on the large window sill behind him. Neither seems to care much about the camera. It's not a suave talk-show kind of scene. He wears a white long-sleeved shirt under a heavy multi-zippered leather jacket whose sleeves are pushed up, and because he's sitting a bit forward from her she looks exaggeratedly small, and his hair—long full dreads that reach halfway to his waist—contrasts with the exposed look of her shaved head. He wears dark tinted glasses, his expression hard to read. She wears a black long-sleeved shirt and what look like black track pants, under a big cut-off chintzy green t-shirt that proclaims, in cursive, *Irish Princess*. She looks elven in the oversized clothes and chair. Later she smokes a cigarette or two, blowing smoke to the side where he's not.

o

At a protest I just attended, organizers urged us toward social media. *Share, share, share.* This wasn't the only action urged: phone numbers of senators got chanted, bill numbers got chanted, one candidate in an upcoming local election was praised, *educate your friends and family and community*, we were told, *talk to your elders, gather their stories…*

The protest was for the liberation of Palestine. The occasion was Israel's latest assault on Gaza, May 2021. In the preceding weeks Israeli settlement efforts had encroached further into the East Jerusalem neighborhood of Sheikh Jarrah, threatening to expel Palestinian families who live there. Ethnic cleansing. Resistance to these settlement efforts mounted, including from Hamas in Gaza. Meanwhile Israeli police perpetrated a violent raid on al-Aqsa Mosque, images broadcast round the world. Now, war on Gaza, one of the world's poorest, most desperate places, a confined area with only four hours of electricity a day, an "open-air prison" which few residents are allowed to ever leave. "Gaza, Gaza, don't you cry / Palestine will never die," the crowd chanted, with a pronunciation I fail at—steadfast hope in response to the despair and mourning anyone might feel upon reading the news.

That week twelve Palestinian children had been killed in an Israeli airstrike in the midst of receiving trauma therapy for their previous experiences of war. 66 children total, murdered, during this week of war. In one family, members of four generations were killed. The only covid testing lab in Gaza bombed, amid nineteen healthcare facilities targeted.

Thousands of miles from Gaza, about 500 people attended this protest, in a small park downtown, by a public sculpture that's an odd local landmark: a huge red stamp that spells backward (as a stamp would, if you were to use it) the word *FREE*. Most people in the crowd were Arab, likely Palestinian, to the best guess of someone glancing around. The event was bilingual: English, Arabic. Black, white, green, red—colors of the flag—everywhere. From the crowd's center, speeches emanated: calls for action, testimony, analysis, alternately addressing the Palestinian community gathered, those here as allies, any and all.

Social media was praised as a vital tool in the struggle. OK. I should learn, I thought, from this pragmatism. This hope. It was hard to hear the organizers, activists, community and religious leaders giving speeches. Police had dismantled the stage and sound system, leaving just a megaphone. Those speaking at the center were standing on something, I think an old war memorial, they were elevated above the line of the crowd. Police helicopters overhead, counterprotestors behind, surrounding traffic, the noise of the crowd together made a thick hot layer that these voices, growing hoarse in the second hour, barely broke through. At a protest people look joyful. Little kids, families who call to each other, older men in button-down shirts gripping each other's elbows or shoulders in greeting. The pandemic was receding, we could draw near each other again, we could shout openly into the air of our city.

What kind of thinking is feeling? I felt no self-consciousness: a rare grace. What mattered was that I was there, not who I thought I was. In a crowd gathered, there is the lightness of freedom as the self vanishes into others. In a protest you think with the protest, free from the dominion of the personal. The noise, the scope and heat and crush of it—you can't comment on it, you are it. You lack irony, your movements are among others and honest.

There are contradictions—your feelings of futility, mourning, and privilege; your gratitude and joy to be present—yet contradictions don't defeat you. In contradiction you go on, with others.

You can't know, as you head off to a protest—as you cut up a cardboard box, open a window to disperse the smell as you write out a sign with a sharpie—what effect, if any, this action will have. The failure of a protest—the 2003 US war on Iraq inspired the largest worldwide protest movement in history at the time, *No Blood for Oil*—is devastating. When a friend's teenage daughter said with regret that she couldn't hear the speech just then being given, by the mother of a young boy in our city murdered by police, I replied that at events like this I often can't hear a thing. "You're just like, *I'm here*," she said, smiling, making a gesture like she was holding a sign, which I was. Am I a hypocrite? I wondered. I'm all concerned about texts and contexts and audiences online—but in person I let voices wash in and out of the lush background, I'm fine when people shout something or hold a sign I don't like, the difference isn't definitive, I don't leave. At a protest people like to attach their personal cause to the main cause (the PETA folks, the surreptitious person with a vague pamphlet saying "revolution committee," the guy dressed confusingly like a medieval knight)—it's annoying or persuasive or ugly or carnivalesque.

Freedom can happen in the gathering of people. I chant "From the river to the sea / Palestine will be free" and I have faith in the meaning I share. Equal rights for all, river to sea, Israeli and Palestinian, equality regardless of religion or nationality. This includes the right of return for Palestinians, those in exile and diaspora, in legacies of dispossession, the right to come home. If I fear how others interpret the phrase—imposing on it an antisemitic animus it does not have—I overcome that fear when asked to add my voice. In the gathering I feel hope for what we have in common. My own smallness is a relief, not a failure, I am just one of many, that's all that's needed. Perhaps others feel this way online. Anyway these days we stand in two worlds always at once—IRL breaking into online and vice versa. *I just want to see*—a friend said, his turn to shout from the heart of the crowd—*all your beautiful faces here today.*

It's not that the place is free. Around the park are dozens of cop cars, hundreds of cops, and yes, our city like many American cities sends its police to train in Israel, to learn "counterterrorism" there and return here. In our city like many cities a Black man or woman, or child, dies at the hands of police week after week, month after month. Our youth are too often lost to state violence, gun violence, and the walls of so many prisons in this state. Our city has been named the worst city in the US for Black women to live.

At the protest, in the gathering, I feel something like—something closer to—another place we may make together, another place that is here. The cops surround the protest but there's a sense of common life beyond them, because we're all here, outnumbering them, despite them, in counterargument to the force they are. This resistance isn't winning yet. But a free place would begin like this, it would be more like this. Online I still feel like I'm performing, I'm looking for those likes, I'm facing outward, needing to be seen and recognized, I'm speaking like a professional whose speech is made for someone to affirm. When I realize the tech companies are there, in an online space—like a line of cop cars representing this power—I think, ah, they've won, this is their space, not mine. The protest feels different. Here we're creating something interior together, something at the heart of the crowd. We recognize one another by freeing ourselves to be no more than one among many. This language is ours. I feel closer to the dream of the place, to the place liberation would be, the language it would need. I don't know it yet, but I feel like it could *be*. The gathering is a kind of place, like the poem is a place, as the Palestinian poet Mahmoud Darwish says (in translation), "the land of my poem is green and high": the poem is the past and future land. In the poem we're not there, but we're practicing being there. We say to each other, you may be there, you will get there. We say, you deserve to live in a present of equality, free in the world we share. Together we want to offer each other this—and the work is at hand for those of us who are here, on the land where we're standing, because of colonization, inheritors of its cruel triumphs, from sea to shining sea. We deserve the chance to work until everyone may be finally equally here. Present in what Peter Dimock calls "an ordinary shared duration from which no one is excluded and from which no one is ever found to be missing." At the protest people want to be there together because they know they can't get there by themselves. Everyone's trying to say what they could mean together.

∘

"And after you did that, Sinéad, in your words, what happened?"

"Um, well, there was a deathly silence, for about half an hour. […] The doors were all closed and all that and they were all screaming at my manager, and that's all that happened, really."

"What effect do you think this is going to have on your career, Sinéad?"

"I don't know."

"Do you care?"

"Well, it depends on what you mean […] You'd have to say what you meant."

○

In 2021 O'Connor will write: "I feel that having a number-one record [her 1990 album *I Do Not Want What I Have Not Got*] derailed my career and my tearing the photo put me back on the right track." In an interview that spring she'll agree that the moment "[defined] her career": "Yes, in a beautiful fucking way. There was no doubt about who this bitch is. There was no more mistaking this woman for a pop star. But it was not derailing; people say, 'Oh, you fucked up your career' but they're talking about the career they had in mind for me. […] I fucked up *their* career, not mine."

She'll write: "'Success' was making a failure of my life […] I gotta get to the other side of life."

○

But in the moment, impossible thickness and speed of the present, knee to knee with life as it happens, as you ask for an ashtray no one brings. In the day-after interview, Lindo is charismatic and patronizing. He's stuck on the question of whether O'Connor did something meaningful. Is she a naïve pop star looking for attention, some half-baked politics that could serve as her brand, or is she a worthwhile political ally and activist? His questions loop around this concern and he has the accusatory tone that is often, and it's a bit unfair, directed at people who've tried to act. Like, *having done something, why didn't you do more, or do everything?* Yet although he's skeptical, although he challenges her, he's not asking gotcha questions. He seems to really want to know: what action would be meaningful and effective? What does it mean to do something, how do you do something that means? Like a good teacher— I'd say—he doesn't ask questions whose answers he already knows.

"Ripping up the Pope's picture may stimulate conversation or it may bring attention to *your* feelings about the issue," he says at one point, "but, as I've said, there have been hundreds of other people who feel and know some of the same things you do. What can all you people who feel that way *do*? Just feeling that way about something and having a point of view is useless if you don't translate it into positive action."

In reply she invokes the exchange they're in: "Well, I would consider this conversation to be positive action."

Later he comes back to the same theme: "Do you believe you can achieve and stimulate some change with what you're doing?"

She points to the influence of pop speech: "Yes, I do. Yes, I do. If that wasn't true than Pepsi-Cola wouldn't want their emblems in the corners of pop stars' videos."

"Are you prepared to accept the consequences […] of what you're doing?"

"What consequences? Look at the alternative."

"What is the alternative?"

She pauses, she looks for language. "The alternative to telling the truth. The alternative to actually getting to the other side, having completed what you came to do, whatever it may be, without having fucked it up."

When he next returns to this theme he's impassioned: "It seems to me a little bit, you see, Sinéad, that your just going on TV tearing up the Pope's picture is not going to change anyone's mind about anything. It's very optimistic on your part, quite frankly, because the powers that we're fighting—I mean, granted any one individual action could immediately spur change, right?—but the devil or the beast that you're fighting is great […] I mean, as soon as you tear anything, they're ready to shut you off the TV […] Just talking about it or singing about it, people have been singing about it […] and the evil empire and 'dem just get bigger—I mean, *what* you going to do?"

"I mean, I think for a start, if everyone stopped saying

you can't and started saying *you can* and started saying *we can* […] If you believe in God, then you believe that you can. There's one way to change things, and that's to put into action, as you say, what it is you truly believe in. Which if you believe in God, surely is the love of other human beings and the belief that God lives inside you."

○

The thing is—you'll have noticed—the common explanation of this incident still gets it wrong. O'Connor wasn't protesting child abuse in the Catholic Church—the scandal as it would break through the media in the next two decades—or rather she wasn't just protesting that. She was protesting the larger cause of this violence: colonialism. When asked to explain, the next day, she talks about the colonization of Ireland and how the empire of Christianity ("the real enemy") betrays the truth of God, God as truth.

She made a global spectacle that wasn't clear. Not easy to understand or assimilate. This gesture—extremely provocative—risked illegibility. And when she tries, in this interview, for example, to explain, she risks unintelligibility. ("People are going to ask you, where are you getting your information?" Lindo interrupts her discussion—of how psychological damage manifests in the descendants of those who survived colonial violence—to say).

She got to find out what happened next. Where she

was now, the day after, and the next. She'd saved the photograph of the Pope her mother kept pinned to the wall. She put it to work.

∘

At the end of the Viddyms interview, O'Connor reads a statement. On YouTube, amid the un-broadcast footage, we see her read it several times: first looking down at the page, strain in her voice. Then she talks through it from memory, looking engagingly at the camera, but partway through she starts, in her words, "fucking it up." We hear Lindo encouraging her from off-camera (he made her practice this; she said she didn't need to practice). Her speech and her affect are intensely serious. But between the second and third attempts, she turns and grins to the side, in a friendly baby voice says: "OK, no laughing, right?" This seems to work, since the next take—and this must be the broadcast—is her best performance.

This last version departs a bit from the original written text, the text she first read, direct from the page, transcribed here:

"My name is Sinéad O'Connor and I'm an Irish woman and I'm an abused child. The only reason I ever opened my mouth to sing is so that I could tell my story and have it heard. The cause of my abuse is the history of my people, whose identity and culture were taken away from them by the British, with full permission from the Holy Roman Empire, which they gave for money and in the name of Jesus Christ. The only hope for me as an abused child was to look back into my childhood and face some very difficult memories and some very painful feelings and a lot of very tricky conversations. I had to have it acknowledged what was done to me so that I could forgive and be free. So it occurred to me that the only hope of recovery for my people is to look back into our history and face some very difficult truths and some very frightening feelings. It must be acknowledged what was done to us so we can forgive and be free. If the truth remains hidden, then the brutality under which I grew up will continue for thousands of Irish children. And I must by any means necessary, without the use of violence, prevent that from happening because I am a Christian. Child abuse is the highest manifestation of evil. It is the root and effect of every addiction. Its presence in society shows that there is no contact with God, and God is truth to me. The Catholic Church have controlled us by controlling our education, through their teachings on sexuality, marriage, birth control, and abortion, and most particularly through the lies they taught us with their history books. The story of my people is the story of the African people, the Jewish people, the Indian people, and the South American people. My story is the story of countless of millions of children whose families and nations were torn apart for money in the name of Jesus Christ. God [*unintelligible*], Sinéad O'Connor."

She says: "That's it. OK?"

○

In 2021 she tells the *Guardian* she says that she's spent "most of" the last few years "in the nuthouse. I've been practically living there for six years." She's referring to a psychiatric hospital in Dublin, whose treatment she credits with gratitude. In 2015 she had what reporter Simon Hattenstone calls "a prolonged and catastrophic breakdown, brought on partly by one of her children becoming seriously ill" and by "a radical hysterectomy." O'Connor experienced the hysterectomy, a "surgical menopause," as wildly destabilizing to her mental health. "Total breakdown," she writes, from which it took four years to recover.

When I read this, I shift in my chair. My worst brain symptoms follow my menstrual cycle, incited by hormonal fluctuations.

Recently I asked a neurologist: will menopause help? My mother's symptoms got better—I add, a little desperately—after menopause.

I'm sitting in the doctor's office. I've just recounted the past twenty years of illness. I clearly want an escape from the pattern I've just, in detail, described. At age 39 I want to count down the years left.

The neurologist looks at me through elegant glasses. This is our first meeting. She's wearing bright leopard-print pumps. In this hospital, apparently, all the neurologists are cool middle-aged women and the fellows are slim young men, nodding. Her fellow seems proud of her like you're proud of someone who scares you.

It depends, she says. Some people get better with menopause. But some don't, and some get worse.

She could have told me what I wanted to hear. Many doctors (many people) would. I admire that she chose, instead, the truth.

○

During the pandemic, classrooms vanished. We didn't meet. We were flat screens split into boxes labeled by name. Most students turned their cameras off and became voices emanating from a black box. An emoji might appear in a corner belonging to them, "reaction." With each update to the program you had more expressive options. You could change the skin tone of the thumbs-up, the raised hand, to approximate your own.

In my house there were four of us, all teaching online. *Professor dorm?* we said. We were lucky to work remotely, safe from the virus. We were lucky to have good company and living expenses lower when shared. At almost any time of day, it seemed, someone was talking, poised and emphatic, into a hot screen. If I paused in a hallway to listen I could learn and learn. Tones and gestures of teaching echoed, inspiringly different from my own, or disconcertingly similar. Like there were mirrors everywhere and you could go nowhere.

On the videoconferencing program that ruled our days and nights (that feasted on the data of our students), you always saw your own face. There, in the corner. Hiding it from view just made you think more about it. You might as well give your self-consciousness some target, fidget-spinner of your reflection. In some classes mine was the only face. A blank white wall behind me and my yellow teeth, nervous comment about the construction next door they couldn't hear, too-red cheeks.

If other cameras were on you might see endless cats moving sleekly across screens, cat butt turned toward you, someone's childhood stuffed animals lined in rows, their Blue Lives Matter flag, a row of bras hanging neatly from the doorknob behind them that you later realized were face masks, underside of their steering wheel as they drove, or the drop ceiling of the hospital where they worked and were allowed to use the computer.

Students' grandparents died, students lost their jobs, they had to move in with a boyfriend or their mother's loud boyfriend moved in. They failed classes at higher rates than I'd ever seen. They spoke openly of their poor mental health. They disappeared from class for weeks or months at a time. You tried and tried, no response. Whatever the class cost to take, they lost.

In the evenings the four of us had each other. We sat

down for dinner.

I learned that the others planned for class more than I did. I tend to plan on discussion, but in a less structured way. I hope to follow where it leads. I want to know what students think and discover where that takes us together. This approach is less organized, more open, and for better or worse it feels that way. It works less well online, with the program's tiny delays, its facelessness and passivity, freeze-ups and apologies.

To think about teaching I'd always thought about surprise and unpredictability. Cultivating openness and readiness to respond. Surprise is a definitive element. Once, in a bar, a student (old enough) said to me: *That's because, Hilary—I've been thinking about this— you are an anarchist*. I had to look away so she wouldn't see my face, the pride and shame of being known.

At dinner, or in the kitchen, on the front stoop or the porch, you could talk through a problem or question, with a fellow teacher, here in your own home. On the one hand, this could feel like you were always working, since the subject of work was always in common and close at hand. On the other, it could come to feel that your work extended from these moments of chit-chat and chilling, casual fellowship, like your work was made of not just the fact but the material of your friendships.

It doesn't feel like teaching, I'd often say about teaching writing, though this is the only kind of teaching I've ever done. *There isn't a subject we're covering. I'm just trying to make a nice space.* That phrase, *make a nice space*, seems humble, pathetic, misguided, next to academic course objectives and aesthetic aims.

Let's imagine. The teaching of writing often fails to be its own ideal, to realize even this modest an aim: *a nice space*. So how do we try? What does this space hope and work for?

Everyone is in a circle. Everyone shares their writing in turn, and everyone responds to each writer's work. The texts that we study aren't from any canon. They aren't affirmed by experts or made by professionals. This, our text, is something someone there wrote. It is taken as seriously as any published book (students often read each other's work with more care than they read published books). Someone's most recent try—their attempt, their form of hope—is read closely, considered intently, appreciated, critiqued. It is treated both as writing that already is—worth reading, worth talking about in detail—and as writing that will be, writing that is still becoming, that may yet be.

The work-in-workshop is made and it is a site of potential making. We must respect both qualities, at once, together. We're gathered round the table the writer is making (to borrow a metaphor from the writer/translator Kate Briggs). This is an everyday mode we're using for art. Every day we think and act in a tangle of knowing and not knowing, fact and imagination, reckoning and potential. We are both ourselves right now and the hopes we dare to express.

As the teacher you are balanced on thresholds between knowing and unknowing, attuned to surprise, possibility of the new. Students might write about anything or bring any subject up, suddenly in the room. You, the so-called authority, listen and respond. Sometimes you must deliver a spontaneous gloss of a critical movement or period of history. You can't be entirely right. It's not expertise, exactly. It's willingness; you are willing to try. You try to model how knowing might start, what forms it needs. How to care for a question.

In a nice space new forms should feel possible. Something new arrives, something new is welcome. It needn't be totally legible or intelligible. An experiment; a gesture you didn't know to see coming; a rupture in the usual modes. Here's the kind of place that can listen and can listen to *this*. When presented with something wild, strange, or unexpected, you don't pretend it's familiar, smooth it back into what's known or neutral. You try to follow it, try to see what could happen. You offer it the fullest of your hopes.

Understandably, sometimes people want answers. They want content. A clear something. A way to write a novel that will be good and that important people will treat as good. They think you can offer this but this is not what you can offer. You could teach the formula to write a kind of novel that follows a formula. But what makes the good versions of those good is always beyond that. It's in how the writer found their way.

In class I often offer an example from my own work, my own process. *In case it is useful*, a phrase I write and say with terrible frequency. Is it useful? I'm not trying to say, *this is the best way*, I'm trying to say: I too am just someone, this is how I tried it, this is how it worked out, in case that is useful to know. I'm trying to be publicly personal. To say, here I am. Please use what I'm saying to say something you want to say.

In the classroom, in the circle, in the workshop, people are listening to one another. It is moving to witness. Ideally this listening is equal in status and time and becomes mutual. People are often kind. Sometimes someone identifies a state of vulnerability a writer might be in and presents a strategy to care for them. Sometimes someone defends a text, unasked, from a particular criticism, just because they feel that impulse. In their writing and aloud people express things that are difficult and intimate, hard to find a form to say, hard to make an opportunity to say. They have painful feelings and tricky conversations. Sometimes people say something harsh, they get angry, they are hurt. Sometimes (not always, but sometimes) there's a way to talk about this hurt or frustration. A form of redress. It is dignifying. Everyone there is a person, like all dead authors are people, and just as importantly. You write something because you trust someone could read it someday. You read something because it feels good to be trusted. Everyone has reasons they wrote their story, their poem, their essay, the way that they did, reasons they made thc choices they made. Everyone is wondering carefully about everyone's hopes and reasons. We really want to know.

HOLE STUDIES

NOTES AND WORKS CITED

WORK, OR THE SWET SHOP BOYS: NOTES

Thanks to Genius.com for help with lyrics. The epigraph is from Paul Killebrew's "The Bisexual Purge," published in *Oversound* 5 (2019), reprinted with permission.

[1] When graduate assistants and non-tenure-track faculty are included, then nationwide over 70 percent of faculty are contingent labor.

[2] Sources consulted in this discussion include: American Association of University Professors (AAUP), "Background Facts on Contingent Faculty Positions," AAUP.org; Dan Edmonds, "More than Half of College Faculty Are Adjuncts: Should You Care?," *Forbes*, 28 May 2015; Colleen Flaherty, "The More Things Change," *Inside Higher Ed*, 11 April 2017; Flaherty, "More Faculty Diversity, Not on Tenure Track," *Inside Higher Ed*, 22 August 2016; Alastair Gee, "Facing Poverty, Academics Turn to Sex Work and Sleeping in Cars," *Guardian*, 28 September 2017; "The Just-in-Time Professor: A Staff Report Summarizing eForum Responses on the Working Conditions of Contingent Faculty in Higher Education," House Committee on Higher Education and the Workforce Democratic Staff, January 2014.

[3] Jon Marcus, "Facts about Race and College Admission," Hechinger Report, 6 July 2018.

[4] Note this statistic on Americans' economic health in the wake of a cancer diagnosis, cited in a 2019 article by Nathan Heller: "A study in *The American Journal of Medicine* last fall found that 42.4 per cent of the 9.5 million people diagnosed with cancer between 2000 and 2012 had depleted their assets within two years" (Heller, "Tell Us What You Need," *New Yorker*, 1 July 2019).

[5] My discussion of Riz Ahmed and the Swet Shop Boys benefits from reviews, interviews, and articles including: Ahmed, "Typecast as a Terrorist," *Guardian*, 15 September 2016; Joe Coscarelli, "Riz Ahmed's Double Identity: Actor and Rapper," *New York Times*, 26 August 2016; Mehan Jayasuriya, review, "Swet Shop Boys: *Cashmere*," *Pitchfork*, 13 October 2016; Grant Rindner, "Riz MC Breaks Down 'Mogambo' on Genius' Series 'Verified,'" Genius.com, 27 October 2018; Ben Roazen, "Our Music's Got Teeth: A Conversation with the Swet Shop Boys," *HYPEBEAST*, 1 September 2016; Carvell Wallace, "Riz Ahmed Acts His Way Out of Every Cultural Pigeonhole," *New York Times Magazine*, 30 August 2018; Ayyan Zubair, "'Mogambo': Riz Ahmed's New Single Is an

Anthem for the Unwanted," *Brown Girl Magazine*, 4 October 2018. Note that the *Swet Shop EP*, a four-track release prior to *Cashmere*, included multiple producers; Redinho joined as sole producer on *Cashmere*.

[6] The word "defiant" comes from the Trevor Noah interview ("Riz Ahmed: The Timeliness of 'Venom' and Creating Defiant Music," YouTube video, 8:16, posted by the Daily Show with Trevor Noah, 10 October 2018). On necropolitics, see also Fady Joudah, "Say It: I'm Arab and Beautiful," *Blog of the Los Angeles Review of Books*, 12 December 2017.

[7] It's right to note that as of July 2019, the masthead of the journal in question includes several new editors and significantly greater diversity in its workforce than when I was there.

[8] Sara Ahmed, "White Men," *feministkilljoys* (Ahmed's research blog), 4 November 2014. Elsewhere I cite Ahmed's *Living a Feminist Life* (Durham, NC: Duke University Press, 2017).

[9] The song's title refers to the YouTube phenomenon "Benny Lava," in which an American added fake English lyrics, homophonic translations, to the Indian Tamil music video "Kalluri Vaanil," yielding this phrase. The Swet Shop Boys present the Indian original in the terms of its American cooptation, re-embodying its viral mockery when they claim they're "hot as Benny Lava."

[10] I say *she* for convenience and as autobiography; anorexia nervosa is more common among women, but it's not exclusive to women, nor to the upper or middle classes, as stereotype suggests. The population of those who suffer is diverse; people who are trans, and members of the LGBTQ+ community in general, experience a particularly high risk of suffering eating disorders.

[11] See Roazen, "Conversation with the Swet Shop Boys."

[12] Himanshu Suri, Victor Vazquez, and Ashok Kondabolu, "Das Racist: Thanks, Internet!," *Village Voice*, 19 January 2010. See also Rob Harvilla, "A Chat with Das Racist, the Geniuses Behind 'Combination Pizza Hut and Taco Bell,'" *Village Voice*, 17 June 2009.

[13] See Roazen, "Conversation with the Swet Shop Boys"; Mick Jacobs, review, "Swet Shop Boys: *Cashmere*," *Pretty Much Amazing*, 14 October 2016; and Mehan Jayasuriya, review, "Swet Shop Boys: *Sufi La* EP," *Pitchfork*, 31 May 2017.

[14] "A sweaty concept might come out of a bodily experience that is trying. The task is to stay with the difficulty, to keep exploring and exposing this difficulty" (Sara Ahmed, *Living a Feminist Life*, 13).

NARRATING FORGETTING: WORKS CITED

Adnan, Etel. *The Arab Apocalypse*. Trans. by the author. Sausalito: Post-Apollo Press, 1989.

———. *The Master of the Eclipse: And Other Stories*. Northampton, MA: Interlink Books, 2009.

Antoon, Sinan. *The Corpse Washer*. Trans. by the author. New Haven: Yale University Press, 2014.

Beausoleil, Beau, and Deema K. Shehabi, eds. *Al-Mutanabbi Street Starts Here*. Oakland: PM Press, 2012.

Bilal, Wafaa, and Kari Lyderson. *Shoot an Iraqi: Art, Life and Resistance Under the Gun*. San Francisco: City Lights, 2008.

Blasim, Hassan. *The Corpse Exhibition and Other Stories of Iraq*. Trans. Jonathan Wright. New York: Penguin Books, 2014.

Carr, Julie. *100 Notes on Violence*. Boise, ID: Ahsahta Press, 2010.

Charara, Hayan. *Something Sinister*. Pittsburgh: Carnegie Mellon University Press, 2016.

Dimock, Peter. *George Anderson: Notes for a Love Song in Imperial Time*. Champaign, IL: Dalkey Archive Press, 2013.

Fair, Eric. *Consequence*. New York: Macmillan, 2016.

Halpern, Rob. *Music for Porn*. New York: Nightboat Books, 2012.

Joudah, Fady. "Say It: I'm Arab and Beautiful." *Blog of the Los Angeles Review of Books*, 12 December 2017.

Leidner, Mark. *Beauty Was the Case That They Gave Me*. North Amherst, MA: Factory Hollow Press, 2011.

Mattawa, Khaled. *Tocqueville*. Kalamazoo: New Issues Poetry and Prose, 2010.

Metres, Philip. "Imagining Iraq: On the Fifteenth Anniversary of the Iraq War." *Lit Hub*, 20 March 2018.

———. *Sand Opera*. Farmington, ME: Alice James Books, 2015.

Mikhail, Dunya. *The Beekeeper: Rescuing the Stolen Women of Iraq*. Trans. Max Weiss. New York: New Directions, 2018.

Osman, Jena. *Public Figures*. Middletown, CT: Wesleyan University Press, 2012.

Rankine, Claudia. *Don't Let Me Be Lonely: An American Lyric*. Minneapolis: Graywolf Press, 2004.

Qualey, Marcia Lynx. "The Literature of Forgetting and Remembering in

Iraq." *The New Arab*, 12 April 2015.

Saadawi, Ahmed. *Frankenstein in Baghdad*. Trans. Jonathan Wright. New York: Penguin Books, 2018.

Scranton, Roy. *War Porn*. New York: Soho Press, 2016.

Shadid, Anthony. *Night Draws Near: Iraq's People in the Shadow of America's War*. New York: Henry Holt and Company, 2005.

Zaqtan, Ghassan. *The Silence That Remains: Selected Poems, 1982–2003*. Trans. Fady Joudah. Port Townsend, WA: Copper Canyon Press, 2017.

NOTES ON METHOD / DIRTBAG MATRIX: WORKS CITED

Bowles, Nellie. "The Pied Pipers of the Dirtbag Left Want to Lead Everyone to Bernie Sanders." *New York Times*, 29 February 2020.

Davis, Lydia. "Enlightened." *The Collected Stories of Lydia Davis*. New York: Picador, 2010.

"Episode 390: Live from Iowa City." *Chapo Trap House* (podcast), 3 February 2020.

Johnson, Jake. "Fueled by Teachers and Average Donation of $18, Sanders Raised Record $25.3 Million in Third Quarter." *Common Dreams*, 1 October 2019.

HOLE STUDIES: WORKS CITED

Arendt, Hannah. *The Life of the Mind*. 2 vols. New York: Harcourt Brace Jovanovich, 1977–1978.

Briggs, Kate. *This Little Art*. London: Fitzcarraldo Editions, 2018.

Chen, Ken. "Ethnicity as Counterculture: Counterculture is a Praxis." *n+1*, 17 October 2019.

C.K., Louis. "Louis C.K. Responds to Accusations: 'These Stories Are True.'" *New York Times*, 10 November 2017.

Darwish, Mahmoud. *Mural*. Translated by Rema Hammami and John Berger. London: Verso, 2009.

Dimock, Peter. *Daybook from Sheep Meadow*. Dallas: New Vellum Press, 2021.

Farrow, Ronan. "From Aggressive Overtures to Sexual Assault: Harvey Weinstein's Accusers Tell Their Stories." *New Yorker*, 23 October

2017.

———. "Harvey Weinstein's Army of Spies." *New Yorker*, 6 November 2017.

FND Hope: Functional Neurological Disorder. fndhope.org. See Mark Edwards, "Why Did This Happen to Me?"

Foster, Diana Greene. *The Turnaway Study*. New York: Simon & Schuster, 2018.

Guccione, Bob, Jr. "Sinéad O'Connor: *SPIN*'s 1991 Cover Story 'Special Child.'" *Spin*, 18 September 2015.

Hattenstone, Simon. "Sinéad O'Connor: 'I'll always be a bit crazy, but that's OK.'" *Guardian*, 29 May 2021.

Hess, Amanda. "Sinéad O'Connor Remembers Things Differently." *New York Times*, 18 May 2021.

O'Connor, Sinéad. *Rememberings*. Boston: Houghton Mifflin Harcourt, 2021.

———. "Sinéad O'Connor's Open Letter to Miley Cyrus." *Guardian*, 3 October 2013.

Odell, Jenny. *How to Do Nothing: Resisting the Attention Economy*. Brooklyn: Melville House, 2019. Odell cites danah boyd, Alice E. Marwick, and Joshua Meyrowitz on "context collapse."

ohyouresilly (YouTube user). "Courtney Love Warning Actresses of Harvey Weinstein in 2005." YouTube video, 0:12. 15 October 2017.

"Sinéad O'Connor Pens Miley Cyrus 4th Open Letter, Says Her 'Media Bullying' Can Cause Suicide." *HuffPost*, 9 October 2013.

Trecka, Mark. "Remembering Why Sinéad O'Connor Tore Up the Pope's Picture on National TV." *PRI*, 3 October 2014.

Twohey, Megan, Jodi Kantor, Susan Dominus, Jim Rutenberg, and Steve Eder. "Weinstein's Complicity Machine." *New York Times*, 5 December 2017.

Viddyms Video Vault. "Sinéad O'Connor Talks About Ripping Picture of the Pope on SNL (Day After)." YouTube video, 27:43. 8 October 2014.

Zuboff, Shoshana. *The Age of Surveillance Capitalism: The Fight for a Human Future at the New Frontier of Power*. New York: PublicAffairs, 2019.

ACKNOWLEDGMENTS

Earlier versions of "Work, or the Swet Shop Boys" and "Narrating Forgetting" were published respectively in *Granta* online (September 2020) and the *Brooklyn Rail* online (September 2018). Warm thanks to the editors and to Jeremy Wang-Iverson.

Thank you to Sydney Landon Plum, to my family near and far, and in loving memory of Terry Plum.

Both this book and I have benefited from the gift of conversation with Emily Abendroth, Caren Beilin, Lucy Biederman, Justin Cox, Jonathan Crimmins, Peter Dimock, Ian Dreiblatt, Sarah Rose Etter, Leora Fridman, Noy Holland, Paul Killebrew, Kate Kremer, Jess Lacher, Andrea Lawlor, Mark Leidner, Eugene Lim, Farid Matuk, Philip Metres, Sarah Minor, Thomas Mira y Lopez, Caryl Pagel, Alyssa Perry, Youssef Rakha, Zach Savich, Roy Scranton, Jay Aquinas Thompson, Pam Thompson, Lindsay Turner, Laura Wetherington, and others I'm fortunate to know. Lindsay Turner's thoughts on poetry and labor were an inspiration. (Only I am responsible, of course, for this book's limits.)

During a difficult time in the life of my family, Mark Leidner moved to the city where we lived to offer his help. An act of generosity I'll never forget.

In a book about teaching I want to thank all those who have shared their writing, presence, and ambition with me as students—I've been honored. Special thanks to Ali Black, Leyna Bohning, Jon Conley, Noor Hindi, Zach Peckham, and Sony Ton-Aimé.

I'm grateful to Jeff Karem and Cleveland State University for their support of my research and writing.

Deep thanks to Jeff Alessandrelli and Fonograf Editions for supporting this book and for sustaining the big dreams of the small press.

1. **Eileen Myles**—*Aloha/irish trees* (LP)

2. **Rae Armantrout**—*Conflation* (LP)

3. **Alice Notley**—*Live in Seattle* (LP)

4. **Harmony Holiday**—*The Black Saint and the Sinnerman* (LP)

5. **Susan Howe & Nathaniel Mackey**—*STRAY: A Graphic Tone* (LP)

6. **Annelyse Gelman & Jason Grier**—*About Repulsion* (EP)

7. **Joshua Beckman**—*Some Mechanical Poems To Be Read Aloud* (print)

8. **Dao Strom**—*Instrument/ Traveler's Ode* (print; cassette tape)

9. **Douglas Kearney & Val Jeanty**—*Fodder* (LP)

10. **Mark Leidner**—*Returning the Sword to the Stone* (print)

11. **Charles Valle**—*Proof of Stake: An Elegy* (print)

12. **Emily Kendal Frey**—*LOVABILITY* (print)

13. **Brian Laidlaw and the Family Trade**—*THIS ASTER: adaptations of Emile Nelligan* (LP)

14. **Nathaniel Mackey and The Creaking Breeze Ensemble**—*Fugitive Equation* (compact disc)

15. **FE Magazine FONO15** (print)

16. **Brandi Katherine Herrera**—*MOTHER IS A BODY* (print)

17. **Jan Verberkmoes**—*Firewatch* (print)

18. **Krystal Languell**—*Systems Thinking with Flowers* (print)

19. **Matvei Yankelevich**—*Dead Winter* (print)

20. **Cody-Rose Clevidence**—*Dearth & God's Green Mirth (print)*

Fonograf Editions is a registered 501(c)(3) nonprofit organization. Find more information about the press at: fonografeditions.com.